Unknotting the Line

Also from Dos Gatos Press

Wingbeats: Exercises and Practice in Poetry

Wingbeats II: Exercises and Practice in Poetry

22 Poems & a Prayer for El Paso

Weaving the Terrain: 100-Word Southwestern Poems

Bearing the Mask: Southwestern Persona Poems

Lifting the Sky: Southwestern Haiku & Haiga

Shallow-Rooted Heart, Poems by Gregory Louis Candela

Circumference of Light, Poems by Bruce Noll

Letting Myself In, Poems by Anne McCrady

Redefining Beauty, Poems by karla k. morton

UNKNOTTING THE LINE: THE POETRY IN PROSE

Poetry of the Southwestern United States
Number 5

Edited by David Meischen
& Scott Wiggerman

Dos Gatos Press
Albuquerque, New Mexico

Unknotting the Line::
The Poetry in Prose

© 2023, Dos Gatos Press
ISBN-13: 978-0-9973966-6-9

Library of Congress Control Number: 2023933631

Unknotting the Line is the Fifth in a series from Dos Gatos Press: Poetry of the Southwestern United States

First Edition

Interior & Cover Design: David Meischen & Scott Wiggerman

Cover Photo: ©emotionpicture – stock.adobe.com

Dos Gatos Press
6452 Kola Ct. NW
Albuquerque, NM 87120
www.dosgatospress.org

We dedicate these pages
to the memory of four remarkable poets:

Loretta Diane Walker, 1958–2022

Mary Dudley, 1943–2023

Elizabeth Raby, 1943–2021

Dorothy Alexander, 1934–2022

Their poems brightened the pages
of several Dos Gatos Press publications.

Their presence brightened every space they entered.

The ride back to Santa Fé was something under four hundred miles. The weather alternated between blinding sandstorms and brilliant sunlight. The sky was as full of motion and change as the desert beneath it was monotonous and still—and there was so much sky, more than at sea, more than anywhere else in the world. The plain was there, under one's feet, but what one saw when one looked about was that brilliant blue world of stinging air and moving cloud. Even the mountains were mere anthills under it. Elsewhere the sky is the roof of the world; but here the earth was the floor of the sky.

Willa Cather, *Death Comes for the Archbishop*

Foreword

At some point in our part of the world, horses slipped away from the Spanish invaders and adapted to the harsh terrain. No one to rein them in—to train them, feed them, groom them—they evolved into creatures of the wild. Mustangs—part horse, part something else entirely.

What happens when a poem escapes from the stricture of the line? When syntax spools across the page, margin to margin, sentence spilling into sentence? Is there a spark of some kind that transforms a paragraph into a prose poem? Does the prose poem actually *exist*—as tangibly as the mustang? Or is it a mythical beast, literature's unicorn?

We take the mustang point of view. We're not sure exactly how to define the prose poem. But we know one when we read one. And it's been here all along, camouflaged among pages of prose, as in Willa Cather's glorious evocation of a Southwestern sky, quoted on the facing page. Read Cather's passage on its own terms. Forget who wrote it. Forget the narrative it embellishes. You're reading a prose poem.

For *Unknotting the Line,* our one requirement was the paragraph. We invited prose poems, flash fictions and nonfictions, haibun, tanka prose, cheribun.

Prose Poem. Well … it's a poem without line breaks. According to *Oxford Languages,* the prose demonstrates "obvious poetic qualities, including intensity, compactness, prominent rhythms, and imagery." Take a look at Lyman Grant's "True Colors" (p. 10); it'll make you a believer.

Flash Fiction. To the definition above, add simply: *a narrative thread, the brief evocation of an invented world.* In "The Kiss," for example (p. 53), Trisha Simone imagines a human-rattlesnake encounter from the snake's perspective.

Flash Nonfiction. This collection is replete with narratives drawn from *what actually happened.* For personal experience rendered with a gut punch, surrender to "Faith and Falling" (p.39). You'll want to read this gem by Diana L. Conces several times; that's the magic of poetry.

The **haibun** is a hybrid form, combining one or more prose paragraphs with one or more haiku, traditionally a three-line poem, with a glimpse that stops time—for writer and reader. The haibun is infinitely adaptable. In "After Memorial Day" (p. 46), Miriam Sagan relies on two lines of prose, an image stripped to the bone, followed by a breathtakingly simple haiku. In "Walkabout," by contrast (p.58), Cynthia Anderson slows the pace of her narrative to include four prose passages and four haiku.

The **tanka prose** includes both the paragraph and the tanka, a five-line form that shares the spirit of haiku, with a bit more breathing room. See "Reunion" (p. 25) by John Milkereit or "On the Porch with My Father's Ghost" (p. 84) by Lucy Griffith. Relish the moment of epiphany offered by the tanka.

The **cheribun** also includes the paragraph but allows the poet six lines of poetry in three separate stanzas—the cherita. To experience the cheribun at its finest, ruminate with Audell Shelburne in "Water from Rocks" (p.28). Three times, the poet inserts a pause in the evocation of a stunning land-scape—to unfold a single moment of the experience.

In these pages, you'll find clear, straightforward narratives and richly imaged landscapes, reflections on personal loss counterpointed with whimsy, with impish humor. Turn the pages. Follow the seasons. Browse at random.

As you explore, don't fret about definitions. Just enjoy what poets can do when they *unknot the line*.

David Meischen & Scott Wiggerman

SPRING

Viewpoint

Joan Prefontaine

We have come here, seeking solace, to stand among the soft striped hills that frame the Painted Desert in northern Arizona, and to picture the rainforest that flourished here over 200 million years ago in the Triassic Period: tall tropical trees and lush ferns beside rushing rivers, where precursors of frogs, lizards, and crocodiles scurried around for food, along with the Chindesaurus, a greyhound-sized dinosaur.

> what we know
> versus what we think we know
> fault lines

Along the trail, chunks of wood transformed by volcanic ash and water decorate the ground: red, brown, orange, gold, blue-green, black, and even a startling shade of pink. In these close and vast distances, we begin to feel unpetrified.

> inside a rock a tree
> inside a tree a river
> inside a river a rock

Joan Prefontaine (Cottonwood, AZ) has worked as a teacher, editor, and nature writer for magazines. For the past decade, she has focused on writing haiku and haibun. Many of her poems have appeared in contemporary journals and anthologies, and a few of her haibun have won awards. She enjoys photography and wildlife viewing in the desert Southwest and is an avid cloud-watcher during summer monsoons.

Slow Dancing with Rio Nambé

Varsha Saraiya-Shah

On the High Road to Taos we hear waters roar, shaping and reshaping their foam beds. Fluorescent sheets of Rio Nambé coiled in the folds of ravines. Bales of clouds shuffle back and forth over the cliffs. Sweeping blue rooms above, in the day's remnant sun, an assurance of our aliveness. One fork to the next, ponderosas still visible for hikers rushing to trailhead. Hills ritually slip into purple gowns. We continue trekking, soaked in their commanding performance. Nothing but sturdy, fearless limbs abound. Their eros absorbed in braiding what's mutable, waters' snowy plaits reweaving, mirth-making. We pause for nothing. We say nothing. Time stands timeless. We watch without a whisper when a thunder lands. Light body surrendering into ranges of Sangre de Cristo. In its domain, nothing may last but the pebbles, the brooks, inky stars at the back of the endless stage, sleepy dust, desert blossoms, pine needles, cacti, fire, the slow dance of the earth.

Varsha Saraiya-Shah (Houston, TX) is the author of *Voices*, a poetry chapbook (Finishing Line Press). Her work appears in *Borderlands, Cha, Convergence, Echoes of the Cordillera, Converse: Contemporary English Poetry by Indians, Soundings East,* and elsewhere. Varsha has been featured on Public Radio and a multi-language/century dance program, *Poetry in Motion.* Poetry lets her practice the art of living.

Judith Youngers (Comfort, TX) turned to poetry after years of educational writing. She enjoys narrative and ekphrastic writing, particularly, while experimenting with form. You might catch Judith scribbling morning pages in her backyard Adirondack chair with a red-haired dog's tail flagging in her face. Her work is frequently featured in the *Avocet Quarterly,* and she's been published in multiple recent anthologies as well. Judith and writing partner Lucy Griffith enjoy sponsoring a quarterly live poetry event in Comfort, Texas.

Into Lands of Wild Horses

Judith Youngers

As he was drifting to sleep his thoughts were of horses and of the open country and of horses. Horses still wild on the mesa ...
Cormac McCarthy, *All the Pretty Horses*

Mystery sweeps through equine bodies of grace, catches us in cascades of color, improbable mists rising from Southwestern mesas and high-blown prairies. Thin spindles carry sculptured torsos that conjure a corps de ballet en pointe in a land that is not ours to hold. Perhaps you roamed, Equus Caballus, with the Comanche, the Ute and Mescalero, gliding through gilt shimmers of drying grama that rustled below the dome of chalked sky. We know that you secret your stories under the fringe of your liquid eyes. Suddenly, you snort and pivot, flick back your forelock to signal your band. How do you wedge your thighs through the rugged cordillera? You brush the chamisa, snag a carillon of coral bells from waving ocotillo with your flagging tail, your flanks fluid, burnished with shafts of high sun glancing off rincon peaks. Are you a mirage emerging from high desert mesas? Canoers report that you cool your hooves, guzzle the water's edge on the lower Salt, the dimming shoreline that surrounds Saguaro Lake, as you graze on underwater foliage. Ranging untethered, you've never been ours to rein in.

> cleansed with piñon breath,
> spirits expand with wild wonder
> faint nickers echo

Leaving a Mark

Alan Birkelbach

The rancher handed her a pair of thick leather gloves. *You'll need them*, he said.

The bar owner pointed to a marked spot on the wooden ceiling and told her, *Climb high enough on the ladder so you can reach. When he hands the iron to you, then push up against the wood, hard. Hold it still in place a few seconds, then rock it back and forth. Don't worry about the burn and smoke.* She shook her head to show she understood.

The back door opened. Her initials on a rod came in, glowing red and hungry. She liked it. This is what she needed.

> branding iron
> her mark a testament
> with every beer raised

Alan Birkelbach (Raton, NM), 2005 Texas State Poet Laureate, moved to New Mexico four years ago. By fate, decision, and luck, his writing life changed dramatically. Alan has written twelve books of poetry, most recently *The National Parks: A Century of Grace,* a four-year project with fellow Texas State Poet Laureate karla k. morton. They took photos and wrote poems at each U.S. National Park, with the intent to help preserve and protect natural spaces.

Carolyn A. Dahl (Houston, TX) is the 2020 North Dakota State University chapbook winner for her manuscript *A Muddy Kind of Love,* produced as a letterpress, numbered, limited edition. Her 2019 manuscript *Art Preserves What Can't Be Saved* won first place in the National Federation of Press Women's contest, and she was the grand prize winner in Public Poetry's ArtLines2 competition.
carolyndahlstudio.com

Frijoles Canyon

Carolyn A. Dahl

When the two-legged ones, vertical as trees, talkative as Abert's squirrels, chatter down the cliffs speaking of hoodoos, pottery sherds, petroglyphs, as if words increase pleasure, the deer lift their heads and sniff the air.

When the noisy ones slam doors on sound-proof cars and speed down the canyon road, the deer rise from grassy hideouts, stretch their horizontal lengths, and reclaim the trails, though all four legs stay ready to flee if ears have deceived.

Deer know silence means survival. The hikers believe themselves predator-free, every animal Disney-sweet, but all day, a mountain lion from the caldera has tracked their laughter from behind boulders, eyed the little ones, trying to decide if they were curiosities or prey.

A black bear, mouth watering for sweets and lured by bells meant to frighten, followed a couple for hours, hoping to rise vertically on hind legs, stagger forward with paws bigger than their heads, and rip apart tossed backpacks for the chocolate tourists have taught it to crave.

In the dusk that gilds the canyon walls gold, the animals have only hours before the clamor of voices return. The deer graze the Pueblo ruins until shadows overtake the stones like ancient spirits. The mountain lion returns to the caldera and its den, while the bear searches the paths for candy wrappers to lick, and the buzzards blacken roosting trees like undertakers afraid to be alone in the night.

Tomorrow the animals will lend their land again to the two-legged ones. The deer will hide in the underbrush, the lion and bear will prowl the paths, waiting, watching until patience runs out.

Milagro, Maybe

Marla Vivoda

When the sun is hazed by dust, it bends in dusky refraction, splashing crimson and fuchsia in the backdrop, already inviting burnt ombré in auburn orange to set a spell. Then you'll spy a silver-haired woman, thin, rocking on her split-wood porch, listening to the Spirit of Milagro as he plays his squeeze box facing her some twenty feet from her bean fields. He cannot come closer, and he cannot bear to tell her who he is, but he returns to play for her sweet cantos.

From the plains, the lonesome lady moved to the hacienda, then to the city, then at last to her small mountain place, where she tends her garden and picks piñons, fishes for goldens and cutthroats. She hikes the trail, submerging in meditations during dark morning hours when the bear and cougar come to lie on her porch. Mule deer graze the field, for no horses live there now.

Reading at night or humming, contented, she angers him, the Spirit of Milagro. Even with his many deceptions and permissions, she stays rooted. Drought and fires, disease and government, thieves and relations nip at her heels. Once, she shook his hand and dropped him to his knees, pulled him up by the shoulders, splitting him.

Angry, the Spirit of Milagro tracks this gentlewoman on her excursions to Taos and Chama, trying to seduce her to arroyos, to glowing blush canyons and pale, shale desert cliffs. Upon his mesmerizing squeeze box, he plays. But she, mighty in strength, settles in place, endures.

The matron bears storms of locusts, mad toads, and slithering things. Who is the Spirit of Milagro?—left in the gravel, but always seducing with sweet music. And she, always resisting in sweet silence.

Ice-Bridge Migrants

Goyo

The terrain dropped. Unnamed, the Sandia Mountains appeared more than twenty thousand feet above the rift, an orphan escarpment of the Continental Divide—so named now—to reveal huge and deep granite-slab exposures.

As the sacred story goes, people arose through the birth hole—sipapu. Later, self-named Diné, the migratory Athabascans from across the great northern ice bridge called those first dwellers Anasazi, ancient enemies.

Corn people thrust up, thirsting for water and sun. Corn people, buried in sedimentary layers above dinosaur bones entombed in huge plates drifting on a molten sea, crashing into each other. Corn people, unnamed first migrants who reached into new skies.

Marla Vivoda (Pueblo, CO) teaches at Pikes Peak Community College and Pueblo Community College—after thirty years of teaching high school and university courses at Colorado State University–Pueblo. Marla has one nonfiction book, *Get Money, Get Real* (no longer in print), and poems in *Tempered Steel* and *Parley*. Her poem "Parody's Child" was the winner in *Vermillion's* sixth writing prompt.

Goyo (Albuquerque, NM) has published two collections of poetry, most recently *Shallow-Rooted Heart* (Dos Gatos Press, 2018). Six of his plays have been produced, including *El Mozo Regresa or The Kid Returns,* for the University of New Mexico's KUNM Radio Theater. Recent publication credits include *Monterey Poetry Review, Italian Americana, Brazos River Review, Abandoned Mine, Circe's Lament,* and *Weaving the Terrain.*

True Colors

Lyman Grant

at the Dwan Light Sanctuary

If you fell through a prism and splashed your secrets upon this floor, these walls, would you pray to return to one clear light? To something simple, contained, transparent? Known but unseen? Bright against the edge of shadow. An uncolored brightness pretending to reveal the real by concealing the self's complications. Sure, we can hide our bloody desire and dour enthusiasm. We can pretend our jaundiced optimism and fertile envy are cloaked in the sheen of compassion. We can hope our sad confidence, kind bigotry, and arrogant spirituality rush by like a wash of clear water over river stones, glistening. But when you are segmented in silent contemplation here, you are splayed like old shaken rugs. You float with dancing motes to silent rhythms. Glare chisels the air like ice, refraction cutting you like shards. The inks of your complicated soul rainbow your naked face, your arms and hands, your clothes. As if spun, you are broken apart, layered. You are the beautiful complication you've always hidden. Stained. You are one no longer. Will you ever be one again?

Lyman Grant (Harrisonburg, VA), an ex-pat Texan, lives in the Shenandoah Valley. He is the author of several books of poetry, most recently *Symptom and Desire: New and Selected Poems* and *ostraca*, a collection of golden shovel poems.

The Company Man

Steve Wilson

As if within words he could contain such silences. They press against his chest in the dark, where he lies again restless, where he considers a spider-web of doubt that gathers in the corners of the room. This is the business, the company man, who offers to his wife the mellifluent flowers of his loss. This is the father, heading for home, who imagines playing catch with the kids—finds himself distracted, tracing his hurt down some cul-de-sac, undone by a thing sure, hard, shimmering as want, light, a thought in a hallway. What he works to express is here: white curtains, caught by a breeze spare and slow above rust-red rocks.

Steve Wilson (San Marcos, TX) has published in poetry journals and anthologies nationwide, as well as in five collections, the most recent entitled *The Reaches.* A new collection, *Complicity,* is due out in 2023.

Chain-Link Art, Valentine, Texas

Dede Fox

Behind the faux Prada store littered with dusty relics, high fashion, a chain-link fence promises intrigue. Festooned with fastened locks, it announces an array of other attachments, questionable as the one worn cowboy boot, bent and wedged between wires above beer and seltzer cans affixed by their ring openers. Down the way swings a beige dishtowel, tied on with thin green ribbon, perhaps in celebration of a newly purchased dishwasher. An expensive pair of woman's sandals dangles under a flipped U.S. flag, not far from a signed and dated stiletto. Sunglasses, keys, discarded stories about a black padded bra, a red bandana. And over there, a yellow T-shirt imprinted with Sully, a teal-furred, horned cartoon character from MU, Monsters University. Coded notes predict future rendezvous. A striped danger sign warns not to remove items from the fence. A child's neon orange flip-flop flips as the wind whispers through dreamcatchers—of human hopes for future lovelocks as colorful and firmly attached as those that line this barren road.

Dede Fox (The Woodlands, TX) was 2016-2019 NEA Writer at Bryan Federal Prison and 2017-2022 Montgomery County Poet Laureate. She currently writes with hematology/oncology patients at Texas Children's Hospital. Dede has a novel in verse, *On Wings of Silence: Mexico '68* (Lamar University Literary Press, 2019). Other works include *The Treasure in the Tiny Blue Tin, Postcards Home,* and *Confessions of a Jewish Texan.* Dede reviews poetry books for *The Texas Observer* and *Lonestar Literary Life.*

100 Untitled Works in Mill Aluminum

Mark Jodon

Constructed on the cracked, mosaic land, where reddish brown shrubs appear scorched or wintered only days away from becoming tumbleweeds, two old artillery sheds with long, continuous walls of square quartered windows house 100 uniform pieces of *fabricated* mill aluminum rectangles, otherwise known as art. How delicious the meaning of *fabricate*—to invent or create, manufacture, concoct, make up for the purpose of deception. Shiny objects flooded with sunlight. Light rays reflecting, refracting, ricocheting, shooting an atomic ball of explosive energy into the pale blue Texas sky. Blinding beauty, alluring, irresistibly attractive.

> kamikaze thud
> on a glass window
> feathered suitcase

Mark Jodon (Houston, TX) is the author of a full-length collection of poems, *Day of the Speckled Trout* (Transcendent Zero Press) and a limited-edition chapbook, *What the Raven Wants* (Provision Press). Mark's poetry recently appeared in *Pensive: A Global Journal of Spirituality and the Arts.* He is an Iconoclast Artist.

Ridges Beyond Ridges

Judith Youngers

The artist writes with light and calligrapher's brush, her raven ink sweeping canvas foreground, highlighting a pearled bowl of Rio Grande to mirror pink-washed western sky.

The photographer moves his lens, stalls on the shifting Mountain Spirit that rests behind inky peaks—a silhouetted montage of ridges beyond ridges lying below billowing foam in the troposphere, an imposing heavenscape. His shutter clicks, captures the holy moment of day fade, then lingers to catch the Mountain Spirit scraping mica flakes off ancient crags, dusting obstinate Mule Ears that protrude into darkening dusk. Who will follow the Spirit rising with slow rowing wings to sprinkle glitter into night's dark cloak?

Judith Youngers (Comfort, TX). Biographical note, page 4.

John Macker (Santa Fe, NM) is the author, most recently, of *Belated Mornings*. Other collections include *The Blues Drink Your Dreams Away: Selected Poems, 1983–2018,* a New Mexico–Arizona Book Award finalist, and *Desert Threnody,* essays and short fiction, a New Mexico–Arizona Book Award winner, 2021.

Angels Sullen over America

John Macker

for Natalie Diaz

Some guy was standing in line at a box store wearing women's underwear for a mask. He complained about the loss of his freedoms in America. I quickly left the area. Maybe one day soon the only mortals left on earth will be empaths who recognize the radical presence of angels like Peter Falk did in *Wings of Desire.* Not just pretty quiet ephemeral things that sigh on your dresser or in rummage sales, not white angels but black angels, angels from Montgomery and Spanish Harlem. Canyon de Chelly. Tarantula wasps are busy angels, not just some handsome Germans reading freedom graffiti on the old Berlin Wall. Angels aren't afraid to handle rattlesnakes, aren't guardians of any particular lapsed Catholic but the one who swallowed my mother's last breath or remembered for my father where he misplaced his war may or may not be real.

The ones who say nothing when midnight approaches the battered carpet of solitude on the rez. Or wrestle with one with muscles at daybreak in order to get blessed. The man wore underwear on his face for no other reason than nothing, no one exists beyond his shadow except the Angel of Death. To Rilke every angel was terrifying—*almost deadly bird of the soul.*

Maybe he she or it is not particular or patriotic and the sky is animated with those who shapeshift in silence and prodded by frayed winds, follow a script scratched into the rivers of sand long ago. I'm sure of it. They will lay you away. I once knew an angel that looked exactly like a sphinx moth. Tiny lawless peace seraphim keep vigil over border crossers and single mothers. Some keep their distance and wash their hands of the rest of us.

Window Watching

C. T. Holte

Tomorrow is trash pickup day. One of the local homeless is across the street excavating aluminum cans from a recycle bin. My next-door neighbor heads down the hill with her dog and waves to the man, whose trash exploration is a regular event. Knowing that my bin will not be much help, as I get my beer in bottles, the can collector goes around the corner with two full trash bags, likely heading for the recycling center.

A speck moving above Sandia Crest grows larger and becomes a plane, with passengers heading to Albuquerque for reasons unknown to me. I am reading a book of short stories titled *Lost in the City*. Whether any of the people I see from my window are lost I cannot tell. Can-man is not. I may be.

> The window is cracked.
> Tomorrow someone will come
> to improve my view.

C. T. Holte (Albuquerque, NM) grew up without color TV; played around creeks and cornfields; had gigs as teacher, editor, and some less wordy things; recently migrated to New Mexico with his beautiful partner. He has been writing for a long time—mostly about creeks, cornfields, and his beautiful partner. His poetry has been published in *Words, California Quarterly, Pensive, Mediterranean Poetry,* and elsewhere, and has been hung from trees to celebrate the Rio Grande Bosque.

A member of the Texas Institute of Letters, **Scott Wiggerman** (Albuquerque, NM) is the author of three books of poetry—*Leaf and Beak: Sonnets, Presence,* and *Vegetables and Other Relationships*. Scott co-edited several Dos Gatos Press publications, including *Wingbeats I & II: Exercises & Practice in Poetry* and *22 Poems and a Prayer for El Paso,* winner of a New Mexico–Arizona Book Award.
swig.tripod.com

Sanchez Dreamscapes

Scott Wiggerman

An old woman, less seer than fortune teller, gazes at me with milky eyes, pokes a twiggy finger at my heart and sputters, as if in prophecy: *Your mother. Alive. Wants you to find….* Adds something that sounds like *Sanchez.* Leaves in a fog scented like rancid oil and garlic. *Sanchez?* My mother would use only three Spanish words: *Mesa* (because she lived there), *sí*, and *amigo* (usually preceded by *your ass*). So, *Sanchez?* A computer appears at my fingertips where I google *Sanchez*, scroll through hundreds of people with the popular surname.

On the fifteenth search page, I spot a *where* instead of a *who*—a ghost town in southern Arizona. Seems like an appropriate place for a dead woman who's supposedly *alive.* A fierce spring sun greets me as I appear in Sanchez, wander dusty remnants of a place uninhabited for more than a century. No sign of my mother—or anything alive, not even a scorpion. I investigate till stars come out, till howls echo down the mountainsides.

Suddenly, I'm in the back booth of an all-night diner called Mesa and Chair. A wrinkled Mexican waitress shuffles toward me with a plate of enchiladas and two folded tortilla triangles, though I never saw her before or ordered. *¿Bueno?* she creaks, as much statement as question. *Sí*, I say, as I can't bear to witness her slow chug to and from the booth for anything else. My mother would have asked for butter for her tortilla—not just butter, but *hard* butter, and *not* margarine. Below my fork and knife, *Amigos 4EV* is carved into the Formica, where salsa has dribbled into the *o*. I eat a sloppy forkful, roll my eyes heavenward, and come back to earth, thinking about how good greasy diner food can be.

The cook behind the counter catches my attention in a tight sleeveless undershirt, *SANCHEZ* sprawled in a tat across his muscly chest, a pair of angel wings stretched behind the lettering. He points to a bicep bulked by hours of pumping weights: another tat, *MOM.* He winks. I eat.

Lepidoptera Grammar, Nearly Extinct

karla k. morton

The morning after as the butterflies were making their great migration I had to speak to her words spilling fast as a thousand beating wings had to speak to her *now* had to tell her through my tears that she was loved and will always be loved and the idea of her hands around a steering wheel scared me into an all night sentinel because the thought of losing her or her loosing pain on another stirred the bones of my blood father long dead from a drunk driver a monarch landed on her like a delicate period at the end of a run-on sentence I could only hope to God she understood.

karla k. morton (Raton, NM), 2010 Texas State Poet Laureate, is the author of fifteen books. The most historic of them is *The National Parks: A Century of Grace,* written in-situ from each of the sixty-two American National Parks. karla's work has appeared in *American Life in Poetry, Alaska Quarterly Review, Southword, Arkansas Review, descant, Boulevard, Comstock Review, Atlanta Review, Lascaux Review, Grub Street,* and *New Ohio Review.* Her nomination has been accepted for the National Cowgirl Hall of Fame.
texaspoetlaureate.com

Plight

Laurie Wilcox-Meyer

A chrysalis hangs from her garden chair. *See the circle of tiny gold dots?* Caterpillar danced itself into jade. I bike home, wings and tears. The monarch's bitter pill in mind. My friend sends a photo of her new butterfly tattoo. *I couldn't wait, I'm pining.* Her tissue is already healing. Eventually, we all fly away.

> a snake disappears
> into my closet
> what may or may not be

Laurie Wilcox-Meyer (Asheville, NC) lives in the French Broad River basin in the Blue Ridge Mountains. Her third poetry collection, *Conversation In The Key Of Blue,* appeared in 2020. Laurie has been published in *Modern Haiku, tsuri-doro,* and *Failed Haiku.* "Immersed" is forthcoming in *Contemporary Haibun Online.* Senryu are forthcoming in *#FemkuMag.*

On the Bird's Thin Neck, a Red Heart Flames

Tina Carlson

The flicker drills a snag, bulldozers pinch the ditch. Once clean-wash breeze. Mule deer have fled, antlers hung in hotel bars. Bluffs flake sand from ancient seas. On a rooftop, crows peck incinerated singe. Are you listening? Wild fields have been eclipsed. Snake hollows, hollyhocks, a circle of stones mark a grave. Iris fields, a brown pond's hospital for the hungry. Thistle, lizard, vast plats of grama grass. Flags of plans across a workbench made of pine. Lemon curtains, red school. Gunny sacks filled with grain. Once my father hung a sun on iron for a swing. We lifted his light to the heavens.

Tina Carlson (Santa Fe, NM) has published two collections of poems: *Ground, Wind, This Body* (University of New Mexico Press, 2017) and *We Are Meant to Carry Water,* a collaborative work (3: A Taos Press, 2019). Tina's third collection, *A Guide to Tongue-Tie Surgery,* is forthcoming from UNM Press. She won second place in *Cutthroat: A Journal of the Arts'* 2020 Joy Harjo Poetry Contest.

Rebecca A. Spears (Nacogdoches, TX) is the author of *Brook the Divide* (Unsolicited Press, 2020) and *The Bright Obvious* (Finishing Line Press, 2009). Her poems, essays, and reviews have appeared in *TriQuarterly, Calyx, Crazyhorse, Barrow Street, Verse Daily, Ars Medica,* and *Field Notes,* as well as other journals and anthologies. Rebecca has received awards from the Taos Writers Workshop, Vermont Studio Center, and Dairy Hollow House. *Brook the Divide* was shortlisted for Best First Book of Poetry (Texas Institute of Letters).

A Boy and Two Magpies,
with Mercy, on the Animas River Trail

Rebecca A. Spears

I am different, not less.

Temple Grandin

His inconsolability breaks into a swell of protest and cascades into the air, bringing down clouds that shadow the trail at midmorning. Two magpies in a cottonwood tree flit down from their leafy cover to *yak-yak-yak* a moment at the disturbance below—then go silent as the child's father hugs the boy close, his calm words like a net to catch the boy's cold-water despair. Will it sink like a rock or float away? I know this boy. If only a single embrace could take away all that anguish. When the magpies fly in to get a closer look, their black-and-white wings signal something I can almost decipher, their calls sounding less like impatience than questions or murmuring mercies.

Cottonwood seeds drift and swirl, silver wisps that easily find us, the way the child's cries—*bridge bridge*—whirl in the air and cover us. My son, still carrying his boy, drifts back toward town. Is the embrace just masking his frustration now? The child's keening, his falling-apart, needs this gathering-up, the way I've seen one magpie console another. What accounts for their gentleness, for the father's gentling, his hands guided by a willingness not to lay them hard upon the child? The magpies prattle their approval, then fly into the pewter sky, their blue tail feathers, a stream moving on.

Out of Commission at Indian Canyon

Pamela Ahlen

Agua Caliente Indian Canyon, Palm Springs, California

A child tootles a plastic flute, woeful little mourning dove cooing the bearded palms, blue-note oblivious to the cranky woman splayed on a loaf of rock, her ankle all twist and knot infecting the gorgeous day—four dull-ache hours not zigzagging the trail, not roaming its upthrusts and down, not sharing the ramble. Instead, his solo switchback to nirvana, her lizard-blink from afar, resigned to ice cream for two, a sublimation gluttony, lip-smacking the view.

Pamela Ahlen (Woodstock, VT), special events coordinator for Osher Lifelong Learning Institute at Dartmouth, compiled and edited *Osher's Anthology of Poets and Writers: Celebrating Twenty-Five Years at Dartmouth*. She is the author of *Gather Every Little Thing,* a chapbook (Finishing Line Press), and co-author with Anne Bower of *Getting it Down on Paper, Shaping a Friendship* (Orchard Street Press).

Sylvia Ramos Cruz (Albuquerque, NM) is inspired by art, women's lives, and everyday injustices. Her award-winning poetry, prose, photographs, and historical essays appear in local and national, print and online publications, including *Southwestern American Literature, Poetry Bay, Choice Words: Writers on Abortion, Artemis Journal,* and *Chamisa Journal. Railyards Trilogy: Poems and Photographs,* multimedia collage work, is in the City of Albuquerque's Public Art collection. Ongoing work includes poetry, personal essays, and the history of woman suffrage in New Mexico.

Riding the Mother Road

Sylvia Ramos Cruz

from Albuquerque, New Mexico
to Window Rock, Arizona, seat of the Navajo Nation

Travel on I-40 is never easy on the eyes, no matter which way you ride it. Well, that's not true. It's only true if you drive into the sun at sunrise or sunset. Well, that's also not totally true. The spectacle of the rising sun in conch or peach pinks against an ocean of nascent blue stops your breath until all is revealed. Like coming through the birth canal. Sometimes babies must be smacked on the rump to make them breathe, join us out here in the trenches. As if they know they'll never be as safe and warm again.

And if you're brave enough to keep staring far into twilight, or foolhardy enough if you're the driver and fail to pay attention to the road, the flash of falling sun against a never-ending dust-deviled horizon dazzles in every human-visible hue (which we know is not every hue there is, as pigeons and mantis shrimp well know).

And not true if you look in any direction at the nearby-soon-to-be-faraway. Mother Earth pierces your retina over and over, gallops at ethernet speeds down your optic nerve to your brain where her bounty transmutes to fields of lava rocks left over from the cataclysm, jack-of-all-trades gnarly mezquite, rogue palomino and smokey-gray mustangs, orange-red canyons of Jurassic sandstone, and all sorts of wild imaginings. The sights are enough to make you cry. Which is just the thing, as the eye needs tears to do its proper work. As I said, travel on I-40 is never easy on the eyes.

    heaven—
    blood, bile, gunmetal gray
    Navajo blanket

The Marfa Lights

Gayle Moran

We sit on the car fender in the spilling darkness drinking old wine marbled with ice in plastic cups. Across the vast flatness of desert, we watch the scattered shadows of grazing antelopes who don't even raise their heads to acknowledge us. As the sky dims, the stars brighten steadily to the pinpoint sharpness of a planetarium.

In the dark folds of the far-off Chinati Mountains, the lights appear—first one, two, then many. They glow within themselves like fireflies, white and yellow and blue, larger than headlights on a remote highway, brighter than an Apache campfire would have been when the first settlers wanted to believe that's what they were. The lights move above the horizon, simmer slowly as if in a primal mating dance, joining and splitting and fading.

We are drawn to these lights as we must have been drawn to each other in the beginning: the sweetness of mystery, the hope of becoming part of it. In the ghostly animation of the distant lights, we glimpse the questions of time and place and being as we must have seen them in each other once when we set about searching for answers together. But our pursuit has been as dry as that of the World War II training pilots who chased after the lights, tried to catch them, only to have them retreat or vanish.

So we return to Marfa again and again and try to recapture the mystery we have become strangers to while the distances in our lives have grown to be as vast and as flat as the desert we look across.

Reunion

John Milkereit

We get away and wait where golden eagles are known to soar over grassland. Burrow holes punch in dirt patches. We return to the historical marker north of Marathon and unfold lawn chairs at the edge of a ranch road. We crack tabs on morning Lone Stars ready to lounge again for hours to see what flies by but not to drink too much, to tap down greed for a lucky flyover. We stop sipping when a dark wingspan unzips the horizon. A cunning suitcase heart.

> Each time I hold breath
> a seam appears from a sunspot.
> The breathing poets
> unpack words at the casita,
> dream of rocks to break them open.

Gayle Moran (Houston, TX) has dabbled in writing activities off and on for much of her life. Early writing endeavors included publication of a couple of short stories and a few poems. She wrote a novel for her PhD dissertation. More recently, Gayle has published poems in *The Ekphrastic Review* and *MockingHeart Review.* She teaches communication skills to engineering students at Rice University.

John Milkereit (Houston, TX) is the author of *A Place Comfortable with Fire* (Lamar University Literary Press, 2022). A mechanical engineer, John has completed an MFA in Creative Writing at the Rainier Writing Workshop. His work has appeared in various literary journals, including *Naugatuck River Review, Panoply, San Pedro River Review,* and *The Ekphrastic Review.*

Jesus in a T-Shirt

Mark Jodon

We arrive a few minutes too late: down the sidewalk to El Santuario de Chimayó the curate is closing the door. Today we will not walk on the dirt floor of the chapel or press our hands in *el pocito* and be healed. Instead, I will lean against the plywood shack across the parking lot known as Low Low's Low Rider Art Place Car & Bike Museum. Overhead, nailed to the shack, a painting by Low Low—Chimayó Holy Chile—a portrait of Jesus in a T-shirt, gold icon orb surrounding his shoulder-length hair, dusk blue sky with silver dollar moon rising, and thirteen red and green Hatch chiles suspended like cherubs around him. His head cocked as if looking down the path to the church, the fixed gaze of his eyes says *C'mon, really?* God speaks in silence and sometimes with tiny, almost imperceptible nudges only the heart can feel. In the silence, I am moved to bend down and press my hand into the dirt at the edge of the parking lot, sensing a quiet voice in my chest whispering *it is never too late.*

Mark Jodon (Houston, TX). Biographical note, page 13.

Bonita Jewel (Fresno, CA) learned to read at the age of three and has been in awe of words and stories ever since. She holds an MFA in Creative Writing and has worked as a freelance writer and editor for ten years. Bonita blogs irregularly, drinks ginger chai her husband makes each morning, and reads to her children in the evenings. She loves it when rain graces the arid valley she calls home.
bonitajewel.com

Growing Stones

Bonita Jewel

I sit in the backyard against the sun-warmed south wall. To my right rests a bucket of stones and chunks of cement—a task I began in winter—clearing ground against the fence to create space for spring lilies and succulents. The bucket is testament to my procrastination in the work of beauty.

We once believed stones grew. After plowing, planting, reaping, then watching the world fall white beneath winter, there, in the ground, stones appeared. How could they not have formed while the ground lay fallow?

From where I sit, I cannot see the lilies and succulents, the sifted stones on the side of this house where I have lived longer than anywhere in my life. Daughter of missionaries, I've scattered dreams across continents. They fell like stones that do not grow.

Now, watering and weeding are a joy, this place to plant and watch life unfurl. I kneel in the soil. My ungloved hands uproot weeds and plant seeds. I kneel before words and seeds, pen and sun.

Today, we know stones do not grow. They have no way to spring up, blossom, drop seeds. Yet in this nation's soil, our first peoples believed stones to be animate. Grandfather and grandmother stones holding stories of generations. Living stones born of earth, touched with divine.

Last summer, my daughter and I walked the beach beneath a westering sun, waves baptizing bare feet. We found a large rock pockmarked with holes, some filled with tiny shells. We brought it home. As I set it in the garden, the stone cracked down the middle. I wedged the two pieces with a third stone, creating a space to fill with a succulent. Stone, shells, plant. Together they pull an edging of light from the sky.

Water from Rocks

Audell Shelburne

He imagined finding some peace, some piece of himself, during this retreat. He expected to slay dragons or at least face his fear of rattlesnakes and scorpions. He listens for voices in the desert, hopes to find his voice, so long buried by white noise, quotidian strife. Two coyotes stroll the still valley, bellies shrunken with hunger, hair matted, molting on hindquarters, backs, and legs. Brown, yellow, and gray blend with rocks, sand, shade. Their shapes appear, dissolve, vanish. The pair melt into shadows as yips and howls fade in the falling night.

> Monsoons kick up wind
>
> pick up sand
> before rain clears the air
>
> washes the heat into clouds
> of steam rising from pavement.
> Ripe prickly pears fall.

He sees himself in this expanse, scars of dry creek beds, so many wrinkles marking time as a yucca rides the crest of dunes, then falls, collapsed in a coil of roots noosed around its dead trunk, its own weight too heavy for empty air. He sees this ancient agave, sees winters weathered in its broad blades, anticipates the wait for a lonely stalk to rise from within its heart and shoot candelabra blooms skyward, this last flair, a final flare, yellow, orange, gold, against the darkening night air.

> A giant saguaro stretches
>
> stored rain
> through decades of drought
>
> the broken ribs, the lifeless skeleton
> remains
> reminds life is for living now.

He was the kind of man who knew the difference between Whitethorn, Sweet, Schott, or Santa Rita acacia, between various agave, between turpentine bush, snakeweed, brittlebush, and plain old weeds. He could spot a common raven in a field of common crows, echo the calls of all the birds. He reads the sky and other signs, slakes his thirst by conjuring water from what seems like nothing, cannot grasp why a man would strike or yell at rocks.

A cactus wren perches

sipping nectar from fresh red tips
of ocotillo blossoms, while quail scurry,

tip their crowns to cool breezes and dust baths.
Clouds mushroom on the horizon,
floods looming above the rocks and sand.

Audell Shelburne (Tahlequah, OK) is a professor and assistant dean at Northeastern State University. He has published poems in *descant, Borderlands, Agave, Blue Rock Review,* and elsewhere. Audell once shared the stage with Larry Thomas and Cleatus Rattan, two Texas Poets Laureate, and felt like he had made it to the big leagues. He is currently working on a collection of poems related to his experience in the Sonoran Desert.

Vernal Pond

Annie Cody Holdren

Above the waterless pond I've found a dome of sticks as tall as I stand: the den of dusky-footed woodrats, who curl inside and listen—as their ancestors did to sounds now past or missing. Two hundred-fifty years ago this month, the Capitán de Anza camped a night beside the pond in near-continuous rain. From his leatherjackets and colonists some Spanish syllables must have reached the woodrats hidden here. Before then, the only language would have been Rumsien—spoken while people collected acorns or sedge roots near pond's edge campsites—now gone like water in dry silt.

> Listen for frogs:
>
> the *rana*,
> the *waakachim*.
>
> They'll chorus
> if the pond
> fills again.

Annie Cody Holdren (Salinas, CA), a life-long Californian, lives with her husband in unincorporated Monterey County. Her professional career has centered on interpreting and writing about archaeology and natural history. Annie has had poems in *Anthropology and Humanism* as well as *Catamaran*. She was selected as a finalist for the 2022 Steve Kowit Poetry Prize. For "Vernal Pond," Annie gratefully acknowledges Linda Yamane, who offered the Rumsien Ohlone word for *frog*.

Jeremy Paden (Lexington, KY) has translated Argentine, Chilean, Colombian, Mexican, and Spanish poets. In 2020, he collaborated with the illustrator Annelisa Hermosilla on *Under the Ocelot Sun/Bajo el sol del ocelote,* a bilingual, illustrated poem about the Central American migrant caravans. It won a Campoy/Ada Award for Spanish language children's books. Jeremy's two most recent books are *world as sacred burning heart* (3: A Taos Press, 2021) and the bilingual *Self-Portrait as an Iguana* (Valparaíso USA, 2021).

On Home

Jeremy Paden

I want to say something as true about home as that ball of dough you left to rise in a shaft of mid-afternoon light. Bread must be left unattended, like a pot of water. The work of wild yeasts cannot be rushed; ripeness, like friendship, will come in time. In its own good time. Those who've learned the kitchen through books, move about the stove differently than we taught by mothers who learned from women whose every recipe was simply: watch me. There are mother-meals & father-meals, a food scholar tells me, the grand production & the daily bread, the need to nourish & sate young hunger means food without fuss or elaborate clean-up. Father-food is for the loafers who can take what time they need in preparation, who can leave a mess for others to wipe-up, scrub-down—*loaf* means bread & indigence & who knows how the latter came about.

Does the German for vagabond, *Landläufer*, sit hidden in the past of this American turn of phrase? Or does it come from the Old English word for servant, *loaf-eater*? Yet, lord & also lady keep this memory, there is the one who guards the bread & the one who makes & kneads the dough. *Home* comes from an Old Norse word that means abode, the place where one lies & dwells; it also means hamlet & even world. In Old Icelandic the phrase that means to be born is *koma í heiminn;* to be far from home is to be far from where you were born, to be native means to be born in a place. You & I are from nowhere born into families that wandered the world & sang of the wonders of heaven, our bodies carry a hunger for strange bread, our mothers brought us each into a knowledge of the world by sitting at tables to cook with women & learn from them their taste of home, so we cook & bake & take with us the tools we need to satisfy the tongue-memory we have for those homes we've spent our lives leaving.

First Spring in Arizona

C. T. Holte

Desert plants bloom wildly while the calendar still says Winter. The sun is pre-heating the valley before the impending blast of the valley summer. Sunrise invites birdsong; sunset calls the wild things; evening summons baskets of bright stars, deep thoughts. The quail have gone to roost and the coyotes are not yet on the hunt. A pale full moon rises as I walk the dog one last time before dark. I am distracted by the silence, forget to pursue the questions of how I arrived in this place and am learning to call it home.

C. T. Holte (Albuquerque, NM). Biographical note, page 16.

SUMMER

Lonely Road

Lyman Grant

New Mexico Highway 104

early afternoon
white stripes laid flat forever
shadows hitch a ride

The drive is straight and lonely long enough he begins to become comfortable with his solitude. Windows down. The wind hums its traveler's hymn to him. Leaving home, never home, is there home? Suddenly, he reaches the edge of the earth. The road descends into canyon. He is not falling, but he is untethered. He is awed by the false geography of his assumptions. He is once again awakened to his fragility. Who would have thought? The layers. The strata. He is being guided down again, yet again.

another chasm
grades and switchbacks
this chosen road

When the road levels and curls a final time, he stops the thing that's hauling him. From red rocks grow two squat huts, a cross. Above knee-high grasses, a rope of wooden beads for prayers. *Mary, forgive me.* Canyon wren echoes. He knows he is not lost, but he does not know why he is here. He pauses. He wanders. He opens. Who made this place, in this lonely but not abandoned land? Who leaves the joy of these plastic flowers? Who lights these *veladoras*, the undying compassion of their saints. Who arranges the angels with their comforting arms for wandering strangers? Who calls this home?

longing calls toward longing

Lyman Grant (Harrisonburg, VA). Biographical note, page 10.

The Complete Idiot's Guide to the Desert

Rich Boucher

If you get lost out here, look around for a mountain and make that your North Star, even if that means the star has to just sit there on the ground. Careful about how cold it gets out here at night. If you got lost in the desert intentionally, then you don't need this guide at all: hand it off to that man over there who really *does* look like he's lost. If that man doesn't thank you, it's all a part of the game so don't get hung up on that. Don't get hung up on the heat, or the way the sunlight here feels hollow and holy all at once. Don't get hung up believing what anyone tells you in the American Southwest, because for all you know they'll wind up having only been a mirage all this time when you finally get up close and find nothing there. If you need to call the police, don't—let *them* call *you* first. If you were born anywhere else but the desert, you'll notice that your first year here is full of disappearing buildings, yucca plants where there used to be things you tried to remember and 7-Eleven parking lots made of needles and spoons and zombies. If you lost the mountain you meant to remember in order to *not* get lost, this means you're lost almost forever and now you have to try to find at least *two mountains* to make up for the horizon you failed at keeping intact. Some towns out here don't exist until you drive out to them. Stay sharp. If you lost the mountain range you were supposed to keep track of, and now you're feeling truly lost and completely covered in sweat and worry, stop worrying. What's the point in that? You'll be found eventually by a hiker or a member of some roving film crew and then you'll get driven in an ambulance to wherever you tell them you came from. Think of the possibilities.

Headed for the Gold Fields, Shep Searcy Observes the Failed Camel Experiment

Sarah Wolbach

In 1891, two gold miners spotted nine camels roaming Death Valley—remnants of a herd brought from Egypt to help the U.S. Army in the Southwest.

I'm thirsty, face down in a mud puddle in Death Valley. I look up and there on the ridge is nine camels. One, two, three, four, five, six, seven, eight, nine. *Camels!* Says I to Charlie, lying right there on the ground along with me, lapping the muddy water with his stupid tongue, *Do you see what I think I see?* His eyes are always open for gold. Charlie lifts his head up, dribbling and panting like a dog. Our dog died from no water just last week. *Looks like Barnum's circus to me,* Charlie says. Later, men in the camp thought we was crazy. But we didn't make up the stink, the snorting, the galloping away.

Rich Boucher (Albuquerque, NM) has poems in *Neon, Menacing Hedge, Bending Genres, Gingerbread Ritual, Fixed and Free Quarterly*, and elsewhere. *BOMBFIRE Magazine's* Associate Editor, Rich is the author of *All of This Candy Belongs To Me*. He loves his life with his love Leann and their sweet cat Callie.
richboucher.bandcamp.com

After receiving her MFA from the Michener Center for Writers, University of Texas–Austin, **Sarah Wolbach** (Santa Fe, NM) moved to San Miguel de Allende, Mexico, where she led poetry workshops for expatriates and taught English to the employees of a mushroom plant. After leaving Mexico, Sarah lived for several years in New York City. She is the author of two chapbooks; her poems have been published in many journals and anthologies.

Aeolian Dust

M.C. Childs

A tincture of Albuquerque's aeolian dust has ever come from Persian deserts. Horses plodding traces of the Silk Road kicked up sand and microbes, bequeathed grit to our wind. The Gobi heats and tempers our wind; the deep Sonora adds tooth, but since the 2030s the air is incensed with smoke from burning mosques, Zoroastrian temples, ancient arcane libraries—smoldering wars. The cavalry of djinn, enraged with soot and CO_2, joined by spirit-stallions from Hopi and Navajo arroyos, raise state-sized siroccos and daemon-haunted haboobs—abusive walls of wind. From over the mesa, between the cinder cones of long-dead volcanoes, clouds of half the planet's chaff and ash scream insults into the Rio Grande valley.

> dry cough short breath
> blasted smoke signals
> the horsemen

M.C. Childs (Seattle, WA) has poems in multiple venues, from *Abyss* and *Apex* to *Utopia*. He is still working on getting all the way to Z. His poetry has won awards from the Speculative Fiction Poetry Association. He is also the author of award-winning design books, including *Foresight and Design, The Zeon Files, Squares,* and *Urban Composition.*

Diana L. Conces (Round Rock, TX) is a Pushcart-nominated poet writing in Central Texas. More than eighty of her poems have been published in print and online journals, newspapers, anthologies, and on a city bus. She is the author of a chapbook, *Blue Skies and Blacktop,* a short story collection, *Temporary Things,* and a novel, *The Golden Feather.*

Faith and Falling

Diana L. Conces

We put our faith in the guides, Jeep wheels grabbing at rain-slick dirt and rocks. Each tire a hand clawing for the top of Corkscrew Pass. Pebbles spray down into treetops, down the trunks, down the slope, always down, down, down. Our guide says he never uses a seatbelt, the faster to escape if we go over the side. Land Rovers descend, single-file, dance with our upward-bound Jeep, metal bodies shimmying inches apart between the mountain and sheer death. Under the lap blanket, I unbuckle my seatbelt. The trail is a brittle thing, edges flaking off, deep craters filled with muddy water, rocks strewn in the path. Sometimes the guides stop, consult. I watch their fingers trace possible routes. Past the tree line, we see the bald iron head of the mountain with a single pale strand of trail wisping across its face. Up we go, almost vertical, holding in breath as we squeeze past rocky walls. I study the lichen growing, olive-green blossoms inches from my face.

And then, whether in hours or minutes, we crest Red Mountain, stop. Three hundred and sixty degrees of mountains, tips white even in late July, shrouded in a veil of approaching rain. It is a cathedral of silence. A guide pulls out a small pickaxe, chips at rocks, while we get as close as we dare to the edge for photos. We stand on stones, smooth, round, shifting as we walk. Down is faster than up, but we have learned faith.

Six weeks later, safe at home, I read of a different guide, different Jeep, different trail, same mountains, drifting ever-so-slightly to the right, finding the edge. The weight of that Jeep, that guide, those Arizona women, their faith, rested just a moment on air, before gravity claimed them, turned them into one large metal boulder turning somersaults through trees, landing on its crumpled roof beside Canyon Creek. The driver was not wearing his seatbelt; the two women were. It did not matter.

Breathe

Janet Ruth

A story from the ashes. In a western forest, firefighters race a blow up—a wall of flame. Some keep running and they are lost. Some stop to make a bed—a space on the ground, burned clear of fuel—then lay themselves face-down in it. They allow the conflagration to pass over them, breathe in shallowly what remains beneath them.

> a bit of air
> the only inspiration
> that lets them live

Ornithologist **Janet Ruth** (Corrales, NM) is the author of *Feathered Dreams: celebrating birds in poems, stories & images* (Mercury HeartLink, 2018), a Finalist for the New Mexico–Arizona Book Award. Janet's writing focuses on the bits and pieces, the wondrous webs that connect us to the natural world. She has recent poems in *Scarlet Dragonfly, cattails, Tulip Tree Review, Cold Moon, Ocotillo Review,* and *Where Flowers Bloom.*
redstartsandravens.com/janets-poetry/

Author's Note: With New Mexico and global wildfires in the news, I was reminded of the remarkable story of the firefighters who survived the 1949 Mann Gulch fire, as told by Norman Maclean in *Young Men and Fire* (University of Chicago Press, 1992).

Pick-Up Sticks

Margo Davis

Even in close-up I can't read the muted weatherman's lips but his arched eyebrows intone, *This, this is serious.* As the camera pulls back, his taut core sprouts limbs shooting skyward, like it's a holdup. His arms flounder left, right, left, as if directing air traffic or tossed about by the wind. His fingertips tickle the heavens, only there's no mirth in those eyes. When the camera zooms in again, he shudders slightly, turning his back on viewers to study their map. Abruptly he faces us, stunned. What lies in the wake of a rare Southwest desert tornado: trees uprooted, homes splintered into pick-up sticks, cars crushed like cans. Ratings upended.

Margo Davis (Houston, TX), author of *Quicksilver* (Finishing Line Press, 2022), echoes William Faulkner's perception that "the past is never dead. It's not even past." Originally from New Orleans, Margo thrives on embellishment, celebration in the face of defeat, and firm deadlines. A three-time Pushcart nominee, Margo has poems in *Panoply, Ekphrastic Review, North Dakota Quarterly, Amethyst, Deep South Magazine,* and *Dead Mule School of Southern Lit.*

Sit Here Awhile

Pamela Ahlen

Sit Here, Sofie Siegmann, 2007, Goldwell Open Air Museum, near the ghost town of Rhyolite outside Beatty, Nevada

The giant sofa squats on yawning sand, concrete mosaic jumbo-jeweled—shards of red, amber, green, blue—regal enough for gold barons, the Borax mule team tycoon. Sit here awhile. Take in the callused land, jagged-edged and jaundice-hued. Picture men berserk for holy gold, a town risen like a hot air balloon, where snakes sleep beneath the heat of day and you, ghost chaser, conjure souls forged with grit and nothing left to lose. Sit here awhile. Speculate. Watch the desert sun offer up ingots of gold.

Pamela Ahlen (Woodstock, VT), special events coordinator for Osher Lifelong Learning Institute at Dartmouth, compiled and edited *Osher's Anthology of Poets and Writers: Celebrating Twenty-Five Years at Dartmouth.* She is the author of *Gather Every Little Thing,* a chapbook (Finishing Line Press), and co-author with Anne Bower of *Getting It Down on Paper, Shaping a Friendship* (Orchard Street Press).

Details

Gayle Moran

There is no wind in this canyon we have walked to and the stark smell of new decay buzzes around us. We dip our hands into the cool water of a spring to drink, ignoring the cloud of dirt that stirs from the shallow bottom. Sitting on warm rocks, hanging our words in the still air, we talk about poetry as if it is a place we're homesick for. You tell me you can't write when you're in love, and you are, with someone whose name you never say.

We look for the snakes the sign warned us about. This is where they live, without fear, among the rotting leaves. You wonder how they know the difference between night and day without having to. I tell you how I touched a rattlesnake once while a man squeezed its neck, unhinging the jaws so that its gaping mouth looked hungry and inviting. I stroked it with one shaky finger, thinking maybe it cared, just before the flat head was lopped off and the scaled belly sliced through, end to end, with one long stroke of a hunting knife. Its watery guts fell like memory neatly into a barrel. Later, I ate the fried meat of my snake, white and coarse, and tasted the stringy detail of muscles that no longer knew how to move.

Our words begin to slow in the heavy air and I take a picture before we leave of you sitting on a rock, mouth slightly open, not quite smiling. I look at that picture now and see things I didn't notice before: the shapes of the leaves, the colors in the rocks, and your face looking at the camera trying hard to remember who I am.

Gayle Moran (Houston, TX). Biographical note, page 25.

Confronting the Buffalo

Thomas Davis

I trailed behind the rest of the Scouts. I shouldn't have, and one of the leaders should have been watching, but it was blazing hot and summer sun shimmered light above the floor of Ute Canyon. We'd climbed down off the rim and hiked the canyon's length to the huge chain link fence between the park border and the Redlands. The water in my silver canteen already tasted hot. I wasn't up to such a long, difficult hike. I'd only been out of the body cast for a couple of weeks, but I kept thinking, *I can do this*—determined to be part of the Scout troop's adventures. When I noticed I couldn't see any Scouts ahead of me, I thought, *You'd better get a move on*. But I was having trouble moving through the heat.

A raven landed on the desiccated gray branch of a dead juniper ahead of me, and I stopped, startled. Silence, not a breeze, not the sound of an insect inside the canyon's sandstone walls, not the sound of talking or laughter. Sighing, I forced myself forward and breathed relief when the raven took off, the sound of wings dissipating the feeling of deadness.

I hadn't taken a dozen steps when I made my way around a clump of sagebrush and was confronted by an old bull buffalo. I could smell his musk. He had a massive head with shaggy, dark brown fur—horns menacing, dark brown eyes glaring at me as heat rose in waves off his body. I stood paralyzed as the huge beast stared at me. I was alone. I was lost. I had a buffalo bull between me and the only people who knew where I was.

Thomas Davis (Sturgeon Bay, WI) has been a prolific writer. He has published two epic poems, one book of poetry, five novels, and one non-fiction book, winning awards such as the Edna Ferber Fiction Award along the way. His book *Meditations on Ceremonies of Beginnings* includes poetry written over a forty-year span, while he was helping to found the U.S. tribal colleges movement and the World Indigenous Nations Higher Education Consortium movement worldwide.

After the Perigee Moon

Susan Nalder

Seventy-two degrees by nine in the morning after a full moon at perigee. What a performance. Just as the supermoon cleared the eastern horizon, it got a five-bottle-rocket salute in the far reaches of my neighborhood. Now under full sun and blue sky, Pema and I, off on our walk in the open pastures. Sialia Mexicana flit among the junipers. Dry cholla stand for nothing. Some grasses ripple gracefully in the breeze; grama grasses bend at the top and nod stiffly, like backwards sevens, all in the same direction. No other dogs in sight. Geometric prints by Reebok and Puma stamp the dirt. Two Gambel's quail bob and dash. Their top-feathers mimic the curl of dry grama grass. We pause as they pass. Are they descendants of the quail that used to run behind the house before the big parking lot of the high school was covered in tar? An orange velvet ant crosses the dirt path. Entomologists say the female is wingless and can bite. The male is twice her size and can fly. He can swoop her up for a ride when they mate, and that's when you might hear them chirping. Pema sprints. She sniffs. Abandoned telephone poles, leftovers from a farm when this whole place was rural.

> wood hollow echoes
> downy woodpecker's tap-tap
> softened by dove's coo

On retiring from a career in epidemiology, **Susan Nalder** (Santa Fe, NM) enjoyed her one lucky stroke: She was invited to a poetry writing workshop led by Joan Logghe. Susan then took creative writing at Santa Fe Community College and the Institute of American Indian Art, and published in their collections. Now, twelve years later, Susan is working on a poetry collection and a memoir; the latter comprises prose, poetry and one-liners. Life begins anew at eighty.

After Memorial Day

Miriam Sagan

New Mexico graveyard—hard-packed dry earth, bright with decorations: American flags, pinwheels, plastic roses.

> holiday over—
> just one old man
> standing very still

Miriam Sagan (Santa Fe, NM) is the author of over thirty books of poetry, fiction, and memoir. Her most recent include *Bluebeard's Castle* (Red Mountain, 2019) and *A Hundred Cups of Coffee* (Tres Chicas, 2019). Miriam is a two-time winner of the New Mexico–Arizona Book Award, as well as a recipient of the City of Santa Fe Mayor's Award for Excellence in the Arts and a New Mexico Literary Arts Gratitude Award.

Mi Tio

Kate Padilla

He wasn't really my uncle. He was cousin to my grandfather who had died in the 1918 influenza pandemic. My father said he was the laziest man alive. One strap on his coveralls always dangled in front of his tobacco-stained shirt. He didn't spit a good way out. He would sit on a felled tree branch to relieve his bowels rather than walk to the outhouse. His name was Timoteo.

Back in our New Mexico village, neighbors were family. They took upon themselves to aid widows in disciplining their children. When my mother was four years old, she was severely belted for performing a miracle. She had wandered into the barn and spied a chick's head pop out of an eggshell. In a rush of excitement she cracked open all the eggs. She laughed heartily with her new-found power when she birthed a fertilized egg. She rushed to tell her mother. A neighbor who discovered the "crime" hurriedly arrived at my grandmother's house, armed with a whip, and "properly disciplined" the child.

Soon after that, my grandmother married Timoteo, mi Tio. Tio was of mild temperament. When he harvested honey without a netted mask, he was never stung by the bees. I saw my grandmother gently comb his hair and shave his beard. He was not backward. He was my grandmother's liberator and the protector of her children. The Mexican sword on the wall may have held his secret.

Kate Padilla (Albuquerque, NM) is a native of Taos. Her chapbook *Apples Rot on the Ground* tells of her life growing up in Wyoming and her ancestral New Mexico home. Kate is a Pushcart nominee and a University of Wyoming graduate. Her career began as a journalist in Wyoming. Later, she worked in Washington, DC as a Senate congressional aide. In retirement, Kate devotes her time to travel, poetry, and pursuing her art.

The Poetry in Prose

The Deputy Marshall

John Milkereit

I doubt what the coroner said is true. I pinned a metal star to my pocket and came up from Santa Fe serving legal papers. The emperor's mansion possessed hundreds of lilac bushes, timber and vigas hauled in. Cottonwoods. July's afternoon eye pierced the hot springs orange. Flies swarmed the screen door. I entered his Spanish-style hacienda. I found the swollen body blanketed in a cot cut near the collarbone. I do not believe Lobo, one of his Alsatian guard dogs, chewed off his head. A witness had her mouth closed in an oil painting, the one lured and migrated to this wall. The emperor was probably a con. Phony deeds and shady deals. Dark shadowy clouds over dentures and jewelry. Doc Martin never got paid. White sheets of the autopsy report curled crisp in a kiva. Bullets found in his chest is a good story, no? Did the emperor blaze a trail to Mexico or Italy? I'll never know. Thick grass blades have a mystery voice for the flagstones. His other police dog, tied up in the backyard, spoke until he was shot. Sometimes truth is trapped in a mystic mine.

Unknotting the Line

John Milkereit (Houston, Texas). Biographical note, page 25.

Who to Trust

Lucy Griffith

Augusta's known widely as a judge of character. She can spend ten minutes with you—size you up. Faster if there's a dog or horse around. As if she can taste it, she senses how you treat others that have less, if you can take blame, how kind you are; if you can hold a temper, how much there really is to you. She listens with her whole body, alert, receptive. Lets you talk, reveal yourself. She knows if a woman wanting to work will make a hand. She sees whether that horse trader's hiding something. She's got handshake deals with the well man, the farrier, the feedlot partner in Oklahoma. Thousands of calves and dollars have passed between them. She knows the border code: don't ask questions of someone on foot, assume the best. At the campshack on the far fence, it's her rule: waystation doors are never locked and always stocked. A jug of water, on the cot a folded towel, holding cans of beans and stew.

> a row of horseshoes
> welded to a rack
> chaps hang
> like stories
> leather shiny at the knees

Lucy Griffith (Comfort, TX) lives beside the Guadalupe River. As a retired psychologist, she explored the imagined life of the Burro Lady of West Texas in her debut collection, *We Make a Tiny Herd,* earning both the Wrangler and Willa Prizes. Her second collection, *Wingbeat Atlas,* was published by FlowerSong Press. Lucy has been a Bread Loaf scholar and a Certified Master Naturalist. She is happiest on a tractor named Mabel lucygriffithwriter.com

One Summer, Some Woods

Neil Ellis Orts

Among the trees, you walk through blades of burning light and hot shade. You are alone and among multitudes. Blue jays shout. Cicadas throb. Unseen in the yaupon-thick underbrush, one rodent or another rustles. The pine is lightning in your nostrils. The decay of last year's oak leaves is balm for the shock. You sweat. So many sensations—

Surrender.

With flesh like breath, you are mist, wind, cloud, thunderstorm. Dissolve, condemned and set free.

Neil Ellis Orts (Houston, TX) was born and raised in Central Texas. His work has appeared in a number of small press journals and anthologies. He has published a novella, *Cary and John.*
neilellisorts.com

Mary Margaret Dougherty (George West, TX) grew up in a ranching-rodeoing family. South Texas—the place and its people, where she has lived most of her life—inspires her poems, which have appeared in periodicals such as *English Journal, Red River Review,* and *Texas Poetry Calendar.* Mary Margaret also has work in two anthologies—*From Texas to Montana: Authentic Cowboy Poetry and Stories of Ranch Life* and *Big Land, Big Sky, Big Hair: Best of the Texas Poetry Calendar.*

Bob's Cowboys

Mary Margaret Dougherty

Bob was hard up for cowboys that summer day. Like any good cattleman, he used what resources he had: Amado, an aging Mexican brush hand, and four little kids who ranged in age from four to six: Bob's two sons and his brother's two kids.

Bob and his crew saddled up at the barn. Fortunately, the kids had been riding since before they could walk, and the horses were seasoned brush horses. Except for one—a cutting horse named Hollywood Anne. Bob's niece, the one little girl in the crew, was the oldest of the kids and the one riding the arena mare. Hollywood Anne proudly traveled a couple of miles from the barn with the veteran ranch horses. Because she knew cattle well, the mare wasn't afraid of her job, but she wasn't used to brush. It seemed every step she took, a thorn poked into her legs or scratched her.

Finding and gathering the cattle went about as smoothly as could be expected, considering Bob's crew. They gathered more cows than they lost and turned the herd toward the pasture adjoining the pens.

On the way, though, Hollywood rebelled against the harsh brush and bolted for the barn, carrying a scared, crying little girl. Across the open part of the pasture, they flew away from brush and cattle. To no avail, the little girl tried with all her might to stop her runaway mare. Until, from out of nowhere Amado appeared and ended Hollywood's attempted escape.

Wiping her eyes on her pearl-snap shirt, the little girl took control of Hollywood again and followed Amado back to the herd. Bob, his little cowhands, and Amado successfully drove the herd to the pens.

For Bob, this day turned out well—better, anyway, than the day the same group of kids was riding around the ranch in the back of his pickup. The kids had recently read about Hansel and Gretel and their trail of pebbles. They left a trail, all right—of fence staples.

No One Hugs the Bull

Carolyn A. Dahl

The towering bull lowers his head next to hers. His hot breath sweeps across her face as his nose ring clangs against the block of salt. She shouldn't be here—down on all fours, licking dirty salt, pretending to be a cow next to a bull who could kill her.

How did this bull, big as a buffalo, sneak up on her? He could hook her with one horn, toss her small body into the cactus patch like a prairie dog.

His muscled tongue, green from grass, curves into the hollows of the porous block. Her pink tongue flicks up and down quickly like a rattler hoping to ward off a strike. One eye, black as a cowboy boot heel, watches her. She looks down to hide her forward-facing eyes and wonders why he's not attacking. Doesn't he recognize her as the girl he chases across the pasture to the battered blue pickup truck? The one he rocks side-to-side as she hides behind the rusted seats while he smashes fenders, dents the doors, charges again and again in fury.

With her short nose, lack of fur, crouched shape, does he think she's one of his calves gone wrong? A human child doesn't crave cow-scented salt, or risk being near a bull that could break her back with a hoof.

Once, she slipped into the dark corner of the barn where he was chained for weeks and where children weren't supposed to go. She had rubbed his head, spoken softly. No one hugs a bull. Maybe today, all his anger needs is the sun, to stand by something living that doesn't flee, to share a salt block until both tongues pucker.

He blinks, nudges her face with his rough nose, and moves away. She keeps licking until he rolls in the grass, scratching the back no one dares to touch; then she runs like a calf to the fence.

Unknotting the Line

The Kiss

Trisha Simone

Bejeweled and graceful, I dance in the sun. Mountains climb toward the heavens, crest, then cascade like ocean waves.

I write a love letter on the earth with my sinuous curves. This is my offering to the day.

A butterfly bush mists the air with nectar. Basking in the honeyed scent of her fragrant flowers, I hide. Bashful and timid, I slither to the side. You come closer, so I play my castanets. The parched ground vibrates beneath us with each of your steps. You defile my missive with careless feet.

You tread on me, so I kiss you with my teeth. Receive this gift of venom.

Carolyn A. Dahl (Houston, TX). Biographical note, page 6.

Trisha Simone (Scottsdale, AZ) has been writing stories since her Brooklyn childhood. Poetry came later, during adolescence in Jamaica. Trisha still treasures a few manuscripts typed on yellowing paper. Scottsdale has been her home for almost a decade. When not practicing medicine, she writes about science and health.

Our Lacuna

Ida Moreno Chavira

I remember barefoot cartwheels, knee-stained blue jeans, a yellow water sprinkler and giggles. Young sunflowers reached for the sun. They reached, reached, reached.

We had a tree of pretty, fuzzy, duraznos—peaches the color of early sunrises. Polly and I picked and bit, sucked and slurped as the juice ran down our chins. We played under the shade of the piñata tree—the oak that grew big enough to hold birthday mâchés filled with candies and memories. We made promises and told secrets.

Grandma Mary watched us from the window. Her cigarette dangled from her lips, its ash tail begging to be flicked. Flick. Flick. Flick. Nature's finger pushed us forward. Something yet to be named pulling us away—like the sweet honeysuckle climbing over the fence compelling us to follow.

The whimsy of wishes Grandma whispered to her roses, the universe granted willfully, wildly, hermosamente. Each petal that didn't fall added to the bloom. Each loose semilla carried when the wind blew to blossom somewhere new where the soil was good. On Grandma's shoulders we sought new land. With Grandma's blessing Polly tilted her chin, lifted her arms, and caught the air above us. Fissures filled the open skies with paths she mapped. I cheered her from below, planted firmly with cacti, lantanas, and ocotillo.

Grandma always said, *Aunque tus pies se vayan, tus raíces siempre estarán aquí*—though our feet may leave, our roots would always be there. But when Grandma died, Polly took flight completely untethered. The strength of her wings, I knew, was a gift not to be tamed. The cadence of time crept and carved and quietly clefted a lacuna. Our lacuna. The unhappened life we could have filled it with. The happened life we could have shared. The past tense of us grows smaller—a tiny overlap between two worlds as different as earth and sky.

Now an aged sunflower, I live more in memories than I do of todays. I reach for you, Polly. Do you remember the green grass at our feet? Do you think of me? I wish a piece of you could have stayed, stayed, stayed.

Ida Moreno Chavira (El Paso, TX) has published several short stories, receiving recognition in the *Huffington Post* and *Writers Digest* for her work. Her poems have appeared in the *Texas Poetry Calendar.* Ida loves her family, her friends, and her hometown of El Paso.

Big Chino Wash

Nancy Fine

God gathered me up and wrapped me in Northern Arizona crust and sky. Sixteen and suffocating in loneliness, I sought out spicy juniper shelter, gritty lava-sand warmth, lizards, and the company of amber light as it inched across time-pressed landforms.

Three years later, when Dad passed away, I lit a candle and nestled it in a nook guarded by sharp lava chunks. There, I stared across Chino's sandy belly as salty pockmarks formed in the sand alongside ant lion dens.

Monsoon thunderstorms cracked thunder and curtained rain, enriching my parched marrow. Big Chino's winds sculpted new contours within me, removing, shifting and depositing things in my life. When grief threatened to swallow me whole, Chino offered sunset colors mashed together in wounded purple and neon orange. The sky-wide collage flooded my eyes and demanded, *Live!*

On a ridge above Dad's candle, a herd of deer were bedded down, until three friends and I stumbled onto them. We each ran for a tree. The deer just ran. Everywhere. Into each other, and then they were gone. Whispers of Hualapai footsteps blew across the deer tracks. The wind carried train whistles from the Fort Rock Road crossing, and rubber tires hummed on old Route 66.

Later I left thank you notes in teenage-girl boot prints on the sandy soil of the ancient drainage. And Big Chino left me a sturdy emotional sinew that, decades later, still holds.

Remnants

Bonita Jewel

Joshua trees give way to cacti, remnants of remembered spring ebbing to parched sand as we steer into a sparse rest area. Signs warn us to watch for bees, desperate for liquid in this space where even flesh on bone feels extravagant. A car pulls out and bees swarm a circle of liquid left behind—coolant or motor oil or perhaps, hopefully, water. Yet it seeps into gravel too quickly to quench even the thirst of these tiny, winged things. Bees light on our car, crawl over transparent glass bordering this body from desert. I sip from my water bottle wishing I could push open the door and pour every drop into the ground. I want to revive the waning desert, its only sign of life, water-starved bees. If some prophet's eyes looked out on this dry stretch, would they see bones no springs of water can slake? Or would they believe even dry bones may revive, form sinew and rise?

Several decades past sixteen, **Nancy Fine** (Burns, OR) still enjoys lizards and feels at home in the Big Chino Wash country. Currently living in arid Eastern Oregon, she writes from the northwestern edge of the Great Basin. Published in fiction and nonfiction, Nancy has a poem in *Bearing the Mask: Southwestern Persona Poems* (Dos Gatos Press, 2016). She is at work on a poetry collection intended to encourage folks when they walk the shadowlands of grief.

Bonita Jewel (Fresno, CA) . Biographical note, page 26.

Walkabout

Cynthia Anderson

During the Summer of Love, my family flew west to visit my grandparents at their new home in Sedona, Arizona. Vortexes weren't popular yet, and the red rock landscape lay mostly undeveloped. Bordering an old movie set, their street, Last Wagon Drive, petered out with Coffee Pot Rock dead ahead.

> threshold
> the coyote who won't
> look away

One day, my brother and I decided to hike to the rock. Strange how the terrain became rougher as we went, the chaparral denser, our goal farther rather than closer. After a while, we gave up and turned around—but saw no signs to guide us. Of course, we'd told no one our plan and had no water.

> unseen … unheard …
> the patience
> of rattlesnakes

It was up to me, the big sister, to get us out. Scanning the horizon, I noticed a line of power poles. We walked toward them and followed them to a dirt road. I kept talking nonstop to bolster Steve's spirits. When a pickup finally appeared, two men in ten-gallon hats let us climb in their beat-up truck bed and dropped us at Last Wagon.

> black on blue
> a murder riding
> the thermals

By then it was dinnertime, our parents starting to wonder. They took a photo of us nearing the house, swinging our arms like windmills to keep from falling over.

> twilight hush
> the shifting shapes
> of mule deer

Riding the Earth

Susan Nalder

> *She said she felt the earth move again*
> *I never knew whether she meant she felt a tremor*
> *Or whether it was the rotation of the earth*
> Ophelia Zepeda

It's ten p.m. in the gravel parking lot of the La Cieneguilla Petroglyph site. Home to rattlesnakes and lizards. A boulder-strewn escarpment defines the western horizon. Guys in high suspension pickups with mag wheels and search lights tool by in the darkness. They pull in for a look. Engines throttle. My friend and I are there. Lying back in anti-gravity chairs. The trucks pull out. We start to adjust to the darkness.

I hang onto my chair when the Milky Way becomes evident. Familiar constellations twinkle. We laugh, knowing everything we see out there isn't really there anymore. We've come for the Perseid meteor showers of August. Their tails of fire appear as thin white lines across the dome.

Off along the escarpment, an enormous light ball stabs the darkness. It rolls from north to south in my peripheral vision. We both start yelling. *Did you see that? Did you see that! Did you see that!* We are wild as that guy in the glitter suit who stands and pounds out *Goodness Gracious, Great Balls of Fire* on a grand piano. Ours is named for its trajectory. It's an earth grazer. Its vapor trail smears the night with light and disappearance.

> grasses rustle
> everything out there
> is there

Cynthia Anderson (Yucca Valley, CA). Biographical note, page 71.

Susan Nalder (Santa Fe, NM). Biographical note, page 45.

The Joshua Tree

Laila Miller

In California, the papers say, law protects the Joshua tree. Developers build glittery shopping centers and baked parking lots. The Joshua tree is in the way. Bulldozers knock over the Joshua tree. Everything nice and flat.

The Joshua tree is protected because the tree will not survive the developers. Developers build houses, too, for people who want to move to the wild romantic desert where the Joshua tree grows. The people drive from their desert homes and park at the glittery shopping centers.

The wild romantic desert gets drier every year. If warming trends continue, climate scientists say the Joshua tree will disappear from Joshua Tree National Park before the century ends. Developers build solar farms across the desert to battle warming trends.

Solar farms need nice and flat spaces. In California, the papers say, solar farm developers are exempt from the law protecting the Joshua tree. Solar farms must be built quickly.

In California, solar farms produce power for electric cars to park at the glittery shopping centers. Solar farms power the homes that people buy to enjoy the wild romantic desert. Solar farms are glittery, like the shopping centers.

Solar farms have a life span of twenty-five years. The Joshua tree commonly lives to one hundred and fifty years, equivalent to six solar farm lifetimes. One Joshua tree in California is thought to be a thousand years old.

In California, economists say, one-quarter of shopping centers will close in five years, or one-fiftieth of a Joshua tree lifetime. People shop from home more. If people stay at home more, they will need fewer solar farms to power their electric vehicles. If bulldozers knock over the glittery shopping centers and solar farms, there will be room to plant Joshua trees.

If the law protects Joshua trees in California, and people plant Joshua trees in the nice and flat places where glittery shopping centers and solar farms once grew, there will be a nice view in the wild romantic desert for at least one hundred and fifty years.

Laila Miller (Woodvale, WA) is an environmental scientist who writes short fiction from her home on the lands of the Noongar people on the Swan Coastal Plain of Western Australia. Her work ranges from ecofiction to children's fantasy—published or forthcoming in *Flash Frontier, TL;DR Press, AntipodeanSF, Hippocampus, Cricket Magazine,* and elsewhere.

Flotation

Janet Jennings

Don't bother me between the hours of seven and eight at night. I'm at the bottom of my house.

I float here every day. Held just above the earth, I'm new again. The past, the letter that my mother sent, and all those Bible sessions with my father—a great man, pillar of the community, generous to those less fortunate—cannot touch me.

I float alone, float back before the library, before my mother knew—she must have, I see that now.

I've consumed teachings, I've embraced, chased, felt the love, then watched it disintegrate. I've moved, remodeled yet another home, but this chamber where I drift in body temperature, salted water does the trick. Everything until now has been prologue. Glinting mica. A tumble in and out of amnesty.

I float back past what can't be held. A small body—mine. My father's library. I drift away in a small blue boat to an inland lake, the musty smell of books. I fix on his leather-bound browns and greens, his red morocco. I evaporate.

I realize now, my mother must have known.

Once we drove through Arizona, on our way to the Central Coast. I saw a tumbleweed for the first time. It was dusk. The sun gave its last shout of color before it sank. A gust came up and blew the tangled weed, bounding across the road in front of our Packard. The hollowness inside my body trembled. That tumbleweed pressed deep, embossed my soft, rag paper brain.

I've stood in line for a loving embrace, a radiance.

And now I float back, before my mother's look, the look she always gave, her letter, *You should never.* I roll, get on a boat and row. I am rowing in a blue boat to a warm dawn-colored island out on a far horizon. Her letter just before I married at seventeen. In tight blue ink. *You should never.* I row, I row, floating in my salted time machine. *You should never have been born.*

Janet Jennings (San Anselmo, CA) has published poetry and flash fiction in *32 Poems, Baltimore Review, Nimrod, TriQuarterly,* and *Verse Daily,* among others. The author of *Traces in Water,* a poetry chapbook, she lives in Marin County with her husband and twin daughters.

Aspidoscelis Neomexicanus

J. Gallegos

Let me show you how I pray. I stick my hands and feet flat against garden walls and tilt my head up to the sky. Tongue intermittently juts out in the direction of the heavens and though this wall is only so high, I beseech my Sacred King to raise me up and allow me just once a taste of that divine space. My King, I remain here so patiently still, so lovingly in wait, to one day devour my most anticipated sacrament. Let me show you how I prey.

J. Gallegos (Albuquerque, NM) received a Bachelor of Arts in Creative Writing from the University of Colorado–Denver, where she served as an assistant editor of poetry at the university's *Copper Nickel* literary journal.

Skirmish

David Meischen

Up the rise, a clumped juniper bristles up out of basalt. At the base a roadrunner zips over undulant boulders. Hunter's posture—it's lizard season—he pauses, reverses direction, darts again, stops, emits one of the odd, buzzing trills his kin have been making since the Pleistocene. Brief quiet, as if the August morning is between breaths. Above the roadrunner, a flutter in the branches. Raptor wingspan, a glimpse of hawk. The roadrunner darts again, takes cover among low branches. The hawk circles and lights, armed for bloodshed—sharp-hooked beak, talons honed for ripping. The roadrunner darts, hides. The hawk circles, lights. Hide, circle, hide, circle.

> above this blinding sky
> stinger at the ready
> Scorpius pursues the hunter

A Pushcart honoree, with a personal essay in *Pushcart Prize XLII*, **David Meischen** (Albuquerque, NM) is the author of *Anyone's Son,* winner of the John A. Robertson Award for Best First Book of Poetry from the Texas Institute of Letters. *Nopalito: Stories* is forthcoming from the University of New Mexico Press. David and husband Scott Wiggerman founded Dos Gatos Press in 2004. Residents of Austin, Texas for decades, they are happy residents of the desert Southwest. meischenink.com

Steady As They Go

Joan Prefontaine

My longtime Midwestern mail carrier, Ken, was struck by lightning twice on his walking route through our neighborhood. The first time he was hit, he assumed it was a fluke, but the second time, when he found himself waking from an indeterminate period of unconsciousness in a ditch on the side of Greenvale Avenue, he concluded that he had become a target. *Once you're hit, you become a lightning rod,* he warned me.

> zigzags of light
> the familiar script
> on a friend's letter

In Arizona my new mail carrier, Jody, tells me that she once encountered a young rattler curled in the dim hollow of a rural mailbox, and though it appeared to be asleep, she left the box open and departed hastily, refusing to put the day's mail inside.

> mid-day sizzle
> opening my mailbox
> more slowly now

It is true I would rather perch in an easy chair beside my study window, sipping a cup of tea, while my mail carrier navigates squalls, flash floods, monsoons and haboobs—the highs and lows of forever changing weather—to bring me donation requests, bills, seasonal catalogs, and the occasional package or personal greeting. I am not proud of this fact.

> virga …
> words of gratitude
> longing to be spoken

Stamps

Mary Margaret Dougherty

A character in a movie last night said she would *lick the stamps*. I looked over at my husband and said, *Haven't heard anybody talk about licking stamps in a long time.*

I thought of the roll I peel stamps from these days, then backward in memory to living on the ranch growing up and having pen pals. When I had a letter to mail, I left the addressed letter in the mailbox at the end of our caliche road where it intersected with the farm-to-market road—and money for the stamp if I didn't have any stamps.

Yes, I left coins in the mailbox with an unstamped letter. Sometimes multiple letters. If I didn't have the exact amount needed for the postage, I left enough to cover it as close as I could, on the plus side. My change would be waiting for me the next time I went to the mailbox.

Now we are lucky at the local post office in town if we get the correct mail in our box.

Joan Prefontaine (Cottonwood, AZ). Biographical note, page 3.

Mary Margaret Dougherty (George West, TX). Biographical note, page 50.

Dear Brother,

Terry Jude Miller

It is the angriest part of August and trucks from the part of town gringos rarely visit arrive loaded with boys and men. Life-drenched accordion music blares from their cassette players, their voices a roar of rolled *r's* and ending *o's*. The baler has made two rounds and rectangular blocks of hay wait for their eager hands to grasp twine bindings. They fling golden blocks on the flatbed trailer pulled by a fifty-year-old tractor running on its third generation of farmers. The workers do not need to be told what to do and that may be why they enjoy this work so. They laugh at me, the *chico universitario*, who struggles to throw the bales as far as them, men with practiced backs and callused hands. Our cousin pilots the tractor close to each bale, a job you formerly held in this late summer ritual. He looks so much like you, I almost call your name to slow down twice. The fieldhands' voices rise above the tractor engine's cacophony, rise above the trailer whose pinned tongue clinks and bangs against the hitch, rise above the heat of the day. They toss Spanish words for *brother* and *bastard* at each other, slap dark hands to sweat-drenched shirts, and laugh and laugh until the field is barren of bales. We pass the water jug around, then file in behind the trailer and follow it to the barn. The laughter subsides and from the highway we look like a funeral procession of hired mourners walking slowly toward Monterey.

Unknotting the Line

Terry Jude Miller (Houston, TX) received the 2018 Catherine Case Lubbe Manuscript Prize for his book, *The Drawn Cat's Dream*. A Pushcart-nominated poet, he has been published in the *Southern Poetry Anthology, Lily Poetry Review, Comstock Review,* and many other publications. He serves as First Vice-Chancellor for the National Federation of State Poetry Societies.

I Point to the Sign that Says
See Santa Fe in our Open-Air Tram

Roberta Beary

and you say it's too expensive and not even air-conditioned why it's nothing more than an elongated golf cart and we wander through the heat of empty streets waiting for this local bus to take us to that local bus with an hour in between under the dirty yellow sun and me dripping dust the heat creeping under my bra until we find the museum that's free on Wednesdays and the paper towels in the basement bathroom so lovely on my breasts and I take as long as I can get away with and you're by the sign that says *Ladies* you won't shut up about O'Keeffe's series of vaginal flower paintings and I read about Stieglitz leaving her alone to paint in Santa Fe except for the summers when she'd visit Lake George and on the long walk back to the hotel the open-air tram passes and you say overpriced golf cart and I say we could still take it and your lips purse into I'm not made of money and I don't say I used my miles for our tickets paid for the hotel and all the meals so far and maybe you read my mind because your hazel eyes narrow and you wipe the sweat from your sunglasses with your Mets shirt while I stare at the hole in the armpit you said no one would notice and then the tram passes us only empty now and you say what a ripoff and my therapist's words about feeling validated float inside my head and I say yes and you put your arm around me and say we'll take it the next time we're here and even though we both know it's a lie I nod my head like there's no tomorrow.

Roberta Beary (Washington, DC / County Mayo, Ireland) identifies as gender-fluid and writes to connect with the silenced. Their prose poem "After You Self-Medicate with Roethke's 'The Waking' Read by Text to Speech App" won the 2022 Bridport Prize for Poetry. They have been honored by The Haiku Foundation and the Poetry Society of America. Their work appears in *Best Small Fictions* 2020 and 2022, as well as *best-microfiction* 2019 and 2021.

Trip to the Mechanic

Jennifer Jordan

When on the side of the road, cooling down, a car is broken, I say.

No, he says, it is partly functioning at seventy percent.

Most often we disagree about basic things, like our shared reality and what words mean.

He is mad at me for taking my car to the shop. He is mad at me for forgetting his pot in the trunk. He is my husband, long-limbed and hovering. I borrow my mother's car and return to the mechanic. I ask if I can get something in the car. He nods. I open the trunk and lift the cover to the spare tire. The smell of weed wafts out. The mechanic is on to me. I tell him not to judge.

At home, the normally unmalleable tip of my husband's nose curls up, shifting red to white as he lectures me about why I should trust him, not the mechanic. When I gather up our fights, I can fold them into years.

We share memories and corroded batteries—shared insults like pistons firing. We are not who we said we'd be. Did we lie to ourselves or to each other, or to everyone all at once? I am a backed-up assembly line stuffed with loneliness, the past barreling toward me. I feel sad about my incessant need to describe my feelings to someone who has turned his feelings off. I wanted to be better, not a broken-down Chevy Nova of human relations.

What it means to hurt takes different shapes and increases in its intensity. My edges shrink into me, wet clay receding into desert. I am rooted yet fractured, a desert cliff sliced through by spring runoff.

Other Voices

Cynthia Anderson

I heard the language of rocks once, driving across the Sonoran Desert in triple-digit heat—no radio, no air conditioning, windows down to let the furnace blast of air slap my skin. Drenched in sweat, approaching mountains that never seemed to arrive, I intercepted a telepathic echo: two mesas, on opposite sides of the horizon, vibrating back and forth. A felt encounter, like sensing a snake before you see it. I believe anyone who aspires to be whole, anyone alone and silent in the sweat lodge of a moving car, could hear what I heard, and touch the part of themselves that's no different from stone, with a memory as long as a stone's memory, grounded in deep time.

Jennifer Jordan (Albuquerque, NM) is a Latinx writer and assistant professor at the University of New Mexico. She works in the University Libraries, where she advocates for Open Educational Resources. Her creative writing has appeared in many places including *Creative Non-fiction, Hayden's Ferry Review, Sonora Review, Cutbank, This American Life, Coachella Review,* and others. Her scholarly writing has appeared or is forthcoming in *The New Mexico English Journal* and *In the Library with the Leadpipe.*
jenniferjordanwrites.com

Cynthia Anderson (Yucca Valley, CA) has published twelve poetry books, most recently *Arrival,* a collection of long form poems (Sheila-Na-Gig Editions, 2023), and *Full Circle,* a volume of haiku and senryu (Cholla Needles Press, 2022). Her poems appear frequently in journals and anthologies; her work has been nominated for the Pushcart Prize and Best of the Net. Cynthia has lived in California for over forty years.
cynthiaandersonpoet.com

Water and a Pinch of Longing

Morgan Ray

It was so unlike him—to bring her something. She imagined her father's Pontiac pulling over, red dust flaring under the tires, the door swinging open so he could stretch his legs, stand, and scan the windswept hills in evening light, pink and white sherbet swirls set ablaze in the Valley of Fire, a road he liked to travel on his way back home from Vegas. He must have considered he'd get his wingtips dusty but did it anyway—gathered sandstones that he loaded in the trunk and wedged in place with his monogrammed case.

The little girl smashed them with his hammer, sifted sand through the hourglass of her fist, each color funneled into its own jar to store for when scarcity came. She knew someday she'd need to make a pie with water and a pinch of longing, reconstitute that moment in the desert when her father stopped for her, thought of her.

Utah native **Morgan Ray** (Salt Lake City) worked as a scriptwriter in the San Francisco Bay Area for over twenty years. She returned to Utah in 2014, where she writes poetry and catalogues dinosaur bones at the Natural History Museum of Utah. Morgan is currently working on a book of postcard poems.

A Long, Weird Sueño
about Xeriscapes, Hookers, and Frybread

Rich Boucher

I started hitchhiking my way back home from Magdalena around midnight, and about three hours into the walk I forgot where I lived. Stumbling past small brick buildings with blue doors and fearful suns bolted to the doors. Tattered pages from ancient newspapers blew around the corners of the town square while the stars overhead shook and tilted like maybe whoever was seeing them was drunk. I found myself wondering if I actually lived way out where missiles are tested to see if they still explode correctly. Staggering along Route 60 in the dark, the whole time hoping headlights might find me suitable from behind. Thumbing it so hard under the small-town moon that I wound up with stigmata. Broken glass on the side of the road glimmering the moonlight back to me intermittently. Recalling that wherever I *did* live, they had year-round 4ᵗʰ of July gunfire, xeriscapes aplenty, mountains named for the blood of Christ, megachurches next to the Walmart where a pretty hooker named Bree once told me she could only orgasm in French and that I would never get to see that, monsoons the size of a glass of water—and all of a well-planned sudden I misplace a few hours and then my bed comes rushing up to my face as if it missed me so damned much. I should probably tell you that I totally had a *sueño mal* about the end of the world and it was terrible because in the dream I never got a chance to try frybread. I got up out of bed and took a walk outside just in time for a strange morning thunderstorm to begin. I didn't look up; I looked down. The blacktop in the apartment parking lot started getting dotted with drops of rain, but the sky was as blue as it wanted to be anyway.

Rich Boucher (Albuquerque, NM). Biographical note, page 37.

The Amtrak Zephyr

Rebecca A. Spears

We await rescue somewhere between Gallup and LA, somewhere on the cusp of the Mojave and Colorado deserts. We might be closer to Joshua Tree than the Salton Sea, to Mecca than Blythe. We ask another passenger about the time—it could be three in the afternoon, less than half the day left.

The sun, a white disk, its edges smudged, looks to have hung itself in the western sky. Cactus and creosote stretch to the vanishing point. How do they stand in these waves of hammered sand? That jagged line of mountains, pale in pearl and blue—there must be green coolness and zephyrs on the other side.

We step from the threshold into the narrow shade of silver passenger cars, away from ungodly heat inside those metal boxes. There's the conductor there, behind a megaphone. We give him wide berth, and hear *radioed ahead, never broken down in the desert before*. Except now. Broken down. Withering.

My melting thoughts wander to where I ought to be, several hours ahead—to a Spanish mission, a dress withering in its plastic sheath. I was to wear it at my friends' wedding. I see it now, the pale-yellow skirt, more tinged than the sun, not as rich as the desert marigold. Its bodice, the ivory of a blooming yucca. With its batiste panels hanging loose, I would have breezed across the mission's terra cotta floor, trailing my in-love friends.

While I thirst for this, I rummage through my travel bag, pushing aside rice cakes and lipsticks, scavenging for the water bottle I didn't pack. How I wish for a place to cool down. Some dark burrow. Instead, I look ahead, admire the spare landscape of this alien planet—cholla, smoke tree, empty washes, sand, saltbush, saguaro. The only rescue for now.

Rebecca A. Spears (Nacogdoches, TX). Biographical note, page 20.

FALL

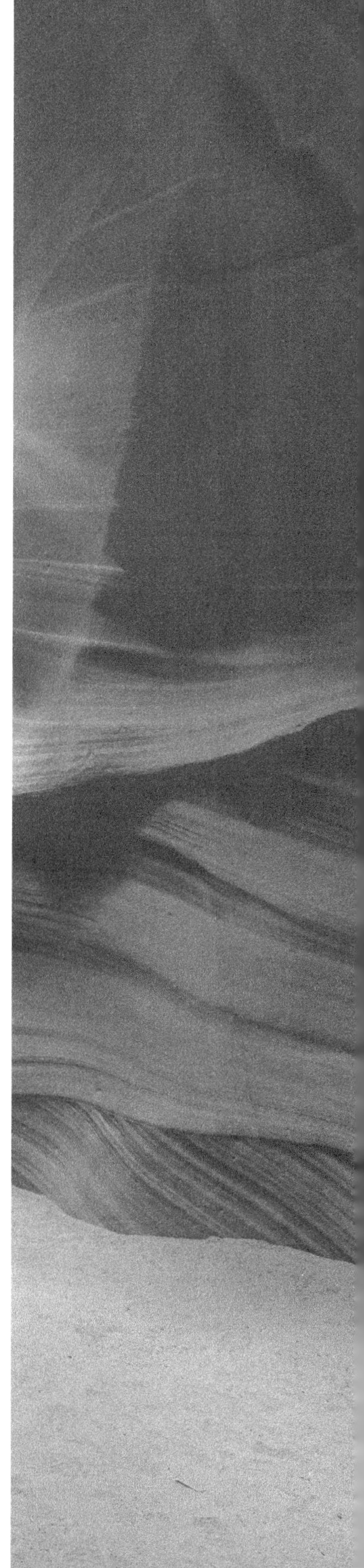

Going South

Cynthia Anderson

I'm at the kitchen window, filling my morning tea mug, when a jackrabbit approaches the water dish. We trade glances, and I look away to give him space and courage to get the drink he so badly needs. When I steal a look back, less than half a minute later, the rabbit is gone. In his place, a Cooper's hawk stares a hole in my head.

> fault zone
> learning to live
> on shaky ground

A lone turkey vulture squats atop a power pole while two ravens sit on adjoining wires. The closer raven hops in front of the vulture over and over, and each time the big bird opens its wings in protest. But the raven keeps going until, exasperated, the vulture lifts and settles on the next power pole down. After a pause, the trickster claims the vacant spot.

> fall migration
> a fresh head of steam
> leaves the kettle

As the latest heat wave succumbs to twilight, I round the corner of the house and nearly collide with a winged thing that zips away. Glancing upward, I find the desert willow swarmed by hummingbird moths. Flitting among the purple blossoms, they are ecstatic, barely heard and barely seen as haze engulfs a pale half-moon.

> shorter days
> the last nectar
> still sweet

Cynthia Anderson (Yucca Valley, CA). Biographical note, page 71.

Mabel's Guests

Janet Ruth

Drifting awake—sprawled beneath an embroidered coverlet upon a strange bed in the Mabel Dodge Luhan House in Taos. In a room named for Willa Cather—one of Mabel's famous guests—I gaze at the white split-plank ceiling. Rising, I hope that during the night Willa's writing inspiration has sifted down through a twist of sheets and sunk into my mind, unlocked last night when I closed my copy of *Death Comes for the Archbishop* and turned off the light. As I tread the floor in stockinged feet, perhaps it is she who points beyond lace curtains. Above the mountains, the sky paints itself in cool silver crests on an ocean of indigo. Extravagant explosions of color wash back and forth among black tree-fingers that pluck at the brightness.

> gilded edges
> Mabel invites the sun
> to Taos

Janet Ruth (Corrales, NM). Biographical note, page 40.

Sharon Suzuki-Martinez (Tempe, AZ) won the Washington Prize for her latest book, *The Loneliest Whale Blues* (Word Works, 2022), and the MVP Prize for her first book, *The Way of All Flux* (New Rivers Press, 2012). Her micro-chapbook is *A Glimpse of Birds over O'odham Land* (Rinky Dink Press, 2021). Sharon grew up in Hawaii. Currently, she lives on the traditional homeland of the Akimel O'odham. SharonSuzukiMartinez.com

Ghosts of Dragoon

Sharon Suzuki-Martinez

In the morning, I found fresh tracks in the sand. The coffee-bean hoofprints of a family of javelinas and the long-clawed pawprints of a lone fox. Low heaps of dirt left by a burrowing pocket gopher. The linear trails of snakes. No signs of a confrontation. Nobody in a hurry. The night before, cold winds whistled through the guest cottage. My husband and I were visitors deaf and numb to the animals living their timeless lives inches from us as we slept. It is their land. And this is also Chiricahua Apache homeland, although not in the eyes of the law.

The light is curious here, making a sunny afternoon feel like twilight. Like a dream only faintly remembered. Maybe it's the way the light bounces off all the smooth, bone-white boulders. They remind me of Surrealist Yves Tanguy's paintings of animate objects. The stones here feel alive: watching, waiting. They are fifty-million-year-old ghosts. Their Eocene Epoch epic patience is unnerving. Do they wait for people to go the way of the mastodons?

Dragoon is another name for a soldier trained to fight on horseback or on foot. The name derives from the short muskets they once carried called dragoons. Dragoon is also a verb meaning *to subjugate by violent measures.* You can guess why this place—Dragoon, Arizona—no longer belongs to the Chiricahua Apaches, most famous for Cochise and Geronimo. The Dragoon Mountains were Cochise's last stronghold against American encroachment. He is buried here in a secret grave. Perhaps he is among the ghosts watching the living leaving tracks in the sand already getting erased.

> upon looking back
> a great gray grasshopper
> lands in my shoeprint

Losing the Sale

Jack Granath

The art market at the convention center unfolds an open connivance between beaver-shaped shoppers and beautiful artists who charge too much. I am swirled along in the current until stopped when the old man rises behind a table and sticks me with his eyes. He is a simplicity of wrinkles and long white hair. He sets a gentle voice against the room's buzz of lust for things, and half a minute passes before I know for sure that he speaks English. He describes God shyly, hesitant to offend, but then hits a kind of mumbling stride and tells me about land leant to the people and promises to keep. He keeps repeating that about promises. He is selling Hopi fetishes—no, that's not right, they're spirit dolls—but I don't feel like a customer now, despite the malachite earrings in my pocket. World out of balance, maybe out of time, a story told in frantic images.

> humans churning
> through an altered landscape
> slow-moving clouds

Meander

Sheryl Guterl

Turquoise sky, punctuated with criss-crossed jet trails and fish-scale clouds, hosts sandhill cranes soaring over sage and sycamore, guided into land by soft glissando calls. Quiet walkers, lost in thought, shuffle through crisp fall leaves, steps like a brushed snare drum, pianissimo on soft sand. River lips murmur praise to the muddy bank, and majestic pampas grass swishes in a slight breeze. Staccato honks of Canadian geese join the percussion of downy woodpecker drills in aged cottonwoods. The bosque symphony decrescendos as sun sets behind watermelon mountains.

spirit songs whisper autumn eulogies

Sheryl Guterl (Albuquerque, NM) claims these titles: mother, grandmother, former English teacher, former elementary school counselor, Albuquerque Museum docent, alto, bookworm. In the summer, she writes poetry from a New Hampshire cabin, surrounded by water, birds, tall pines, and campfire smoke. In the winter months, in New Mexico, lizards, sandhill cranes, and a rich cultural landscape inspire her. Sheryl's recent poems are in *Capsule Stories, The Bluebird Word, Clerestory, SLAB, Zephyr Review,* and several local anthologies.

Casa Grande

Carol Lee Saffioti-Hughes

Cold, she said, as desert wind rose with waves of heat. Two years old, coming from the far north, she knew no word for hot. What was it brushed her that morning, ruffled her sand hair? Late sun behind us, stone notes' lament.

She squinted into my camera, and returned to her pebble, her busyhood. Offered one to me: the throat of the stone, echo upon echo.

I looked back from the Grand House where sun, moon, and stars trace their journeys on ancient walls: light on sacred stones. Small circling birds—Carlos Nakai's flutesongs in my head—the voices of stones rising. Her small voice joined the echoes of found stones.

A year after her death—Autumn Grace her name—a wise woman, friend returned from a visit to this same sacred place, not knowing we too had visited the speaking stones of the Tohono O'odham who were at the monument. I was entranced. As we were about to leave, a small child not more than three, began to dance. All by herself, circling away from the dancers, with the wind catching her hair. Her mother explained, she often dances by herself. Her name, Autumn Serene.

A child's whisper returns: voice of wind, voice of cloud, voice of stone.

Carol Lee Saffioti-Hughes (Mountain, WI), professor emerita of the University of Wisconsin–Parkside, served as librarian in a log cabin in the north woods of Wisconsin. Her work appears in three countries and languages. Her publication credits include *Jimson Weed, The Malahat Review, The Greensboro Review, Poetry Hall, Rosebud, Moss Piglet,* and several anthologies. Carol's most recent chapbook is *When Wilding Returns* (Cyberwit Press).

When the Rains Fail

Gabrielle Langley

All the children will be asked to burn their toys, as in the twelfth century on the plains of Texas. Before the Europeans, before anyone struck oil, long before NASA, Marfa, or SXSW, the Comanche had their own problems. A year of floods swept the plains. Swift currents swallowed tipis, blankets, small animals, seeds, and all the dried venison. Then came a blistering drought. Starvation. Dehydration. The people learned that their gods were fuming, had turned their backs on the rain dancers until finally one tiny hungry girl, an orphan, stood in the hot dusty wind, decided to sacrifice her only toy, an offering to all those angry weather spirits. It was a corn husk doll, beads for eyes, a berry mouth, buckskin dress, and blue jay feathers braided into the doll's black hair pulled from a horse's tail.

When climate crisis comes, children pay the ransom, build the fires, burn their toys, shed their tears in secret. Here, they still teach school children the legend of the bluebonnet, how the state flower first grew from the burnt offering of a child's sacrifice, how she threw the ashes from her small fists to the North, to the South, to the East, and to the West, and how indigo petals are still unfolding from her tears.

Gabrielle Langley (Houston, TX) is the author of two poetry collections, *Fairy Tale* (Sable Books, 2023) and *Azaleas on Fire* (Sable Books, 2019). Winner of the Lorene Pouncey Poetry Award, the Vivian Nellis Memorial Award for Creative Writing, Houston Poetry Fest's Grand Jury Prize, and three Pushcart Prize nominations, Gabrielle also worked as a spearhead and co-editor for the anthology *Red Sky: poetry on the global epidemic of violence against women* (Sable Books, 2016). gabriellelangley.com

On the Porch with my Father's Ghost

Lucy Griffith

Autumn in the high desert, that's when I miss him the most. I sit on the porch of an evening watching the sun fold its tent and slip away. I'm in my wicker chair. Dust billows when I sit. I imagine him beside me in his rocker, boots propped on the porch rail, smelling of horse and motor oil. I see the mountains in his profile, that broken nose from a rodeo wreck. I hear him murmur with pleasure at this year's tall grasses, rewarding us for careful grazing. The little pond by the house has filled, catching overflow from gutters and windmill. Montezuma quail have returned at last after that cityboy blew them away with his itchy finger so many years ago. I feel Daddy's delight at having a house covey again, bustling to and fro from prickly pear to pond with their quavery whistle. A rough-legged hawk lands on the windmill vane, startling us both. It looks like she's wearing feathered bloomers. Don't think he had in mind an all-woman ranch when he left this to me. Mama would have hated it. Don't think Daddy'd care as long as chores got done. He wouldn't know about a bit of girl-love in the dark. I know he'd be proud of the fat, slick cows we've raised and that fences are tended. Pyrrhuloxia, the desert cardinal, lands on the dinner bell, flashing scarlet and silver, hunting the porch rail for seeds. He *che-wee, che-wees* at us with his crooked beak.

> a square
> of olive silk
> loose knot
> at her neck
> dusty wrinkled flair

Lucy Griffith (Comfort, TX). Biographical note, page 49.

The Lesson

Terry Jude Miller

At last, I get it. All those farm field lectures about being tough were really a diatribe with the same message: survive. That time a new strand of taut barbed wire broke from the spool pulled parallel to the mile of fence posts we just laid, wrapped around your khakied leg like a serpent with a body of four-pronged teeth. Tiny scarlet pearls flagged each puncture. You looked up calmly and asked for pliers then cut yourself loose of your tormentor. You smiled into my frightened ten-year-old face and said *pain is a teacher and farmers must be quick pupils*, then patted me on the back and tousled my hair. We went about our duties and finished our fence in the formerly opened field. How many times have I called upon that page of us when faced with this life's serpents? How many moments have I smelled your smoky breath and heard your whispered words as I cut myself free of some aggressor? I stand here fifty-years later, in that same field as the woods to the west wrap the descending sun in their green embrace. I recall the bit of snipped barbed wire on the ground, speckled with your blood.

Terry Jude Miller (Houston, TX). Biographical note, page 68.

Vi y No Vi

Christopher Watson

Vi y no vi lo que ahora veo: la mano tímida de un niño de tres años saliendo de un agujero en la manta—poncho de lana con que mi nanita chilanga me cubrió.

Cómo era?

Era como una herida fascinante, pasaje picante a un cuarto oscuro cuyas características quedan invisibles.

¿Quién sabe que estoy aquí?
¿Quién me cuida?

A última hora de la mañana hay un callejón polvoriento, barrado a ambos lados por chozas bajas que eructan humo de leña por grietas de los parches de hojalata—y el olor de chiles asados acre como laca.

Aquí hay órdenes amortiguados que se dan en un registro incalculablemente cansado ante el ascenso y descenso de voces desconocidas que laten el recinto circundante.

o

Veo ramas y sus sombras iluminadas por la luz de la luna (… *errante en las sombras, te busca y te nombra* …). Cierro mis ojos y veo la oscuridad.

Más tarde, tiro las brasas de un cigarrillo, vigilando sus fuegos hasta que mueren en la hierba del deserto—hierba de la primavera que sigue todavía seca y fria.

Notes:
– *chilanga*—slang for one born and raised in Mexico City
– *errante en las sombras, te busca y te nombra*—a line from the tango song "Volver" by Carlos Gardel and Alfredo Le Pera

I Saw and Did Not See

I saw and did not see what I now see: the timid hand of a three-year-old emerging from a hole in the blanket—woolen poncho with which my nanny *chilanga* covered me.

What was it like?

It was like a fascinating wound: piquant passage to a darkened room whose features remain invisible.

Who knows that I'm here?
Who watches over me?

Morning's last hour, there's a dusty alley barred by low-slung shacks belching woodsmoke from tin-patched cracks—and the smell of roasted chiles acrid as lacquer.

Here, there are muffled commands, given in an incalculably tired register, before the rise and descent of unfamiliar voices pulsing the surrounding enclosure.

o

I see branches and their shadows illuminated by moonlight (… *errant in the shadows, it seeks and names you* …). I close my eyes and see the darkness.

Later, I toss the embers of a cigarette, keeping vigil on the dying flames in the desert's grasses—in the spring grasses that remain dry and frigid.

Christopher Watson (Santa Fe, NM) spent his first years in Mexico City. Christopher studied classics before living between Barcelona and London. He completed his MFA in creative writing at Middlesex University, UK, 2007. He has published in *Magma Poetry, Cagibi,* and *Dark Mountain,* among others; he translates for Santa Fe Dreamers Project.

Cow's Head

J. Gallegos

Grandfather took a cow to the butcher every year. His return excited the children, who liked to feast on fresh meat and gnaw on the bones with their little teeth. When their grandfather returned from these trips, a black garbage bag awaited them in the bed of his truck. Inside was the cow's head, smelly and stiff.

They would dare each other to touch the glazed eyes of the beast, which did nothing other than stare blankly ahead. The brave ones used their fingers to poke and prod while the cowards used twigs and sticks.

The tag on the animal's ear read *Anthony Garcia's Head.*

Look! Look! It's Grandpa's head! They giggled deviously, much like they did devouring piping hot empanadas their Nana made from the cow's tongue.

It's like tasting food that's tasting you!

One day, after the school bus dropped them off, the children found the truck in the driveway, already back from the butcher. They scrambled over, casting off their backpacks as they ran. Hands tore apart the garbage bag, and they found within it their grandfather's head—wiry white hair sticking out wildly at the sides and the bald top glistening in the sun. The eyes were covered by his signature aviators, and a single toothpick stuck out from between his lips.

Wailing for Nana, they ran to the house, but stopped abruptly when they reached the back porch. Sitting in his favorite lawn chair was their grandfather, the cow's head upon his shoulders, attached at the neck. He was guzzling a can of beer, amber liquid swishing over his massive tongue. When he noticed the frightened children, he set the can down.

Lately, my hearing has been going, he said. *So I asked the butcher to swap out the heads for me.* His beige ears twitched as he spoke.

The children gawked at the eyes they would have poked and prodded, but those eyes did not stare back at them. Instead, they looked beyond the children to the enticing green grass in the backyard.

J. Gallegos (Albuquerque, NM). Biographical note, page 64.

Albuquerque Descanso

Dee Cohen

We're used to hot air balloons in the Land of Enchantment. Launching in the early morning, chase crews following in pickups, cars pulled over to watch with pajama-clad kids wrapped in blankets. You never know where one might come down: backyards or fields or roofs of houses.

But not often on streets like Zuni where a little girl was struck by a car a few weeks back. There was an argument between brothers over money. It spilled out in front of their apartment, a crummy two-story building with rusting bannisters and peeling doors right across from a gas station. And the little girl followed. If you lived there, you could hear people filling their tanks all day and the smell of gasoline would seep inside.

There's a *descanso* on the corner, piled up with items: toys and vases, crosses, and many candles. But it's been a while since the child's death and the mound is drenched. Stuffed animals filthy, flowers dead. A Bible a few feet off as if it's been kicked out of the way.

Descansos: remembrances. What should we remember about this scene? The rainbows in the spilled gasoline? The child? Or how sometimes this is the sorriest of towns, squatting down and turning its back, the texture of the morning light as hard as stucco. Oh, flattened balloons clutter the pile too, a reminder to look up. Above the telephone poles and electrical lines, rutted streets and the noisy station on the corner. More balloons rising but from this side of town, they're barely visible.

Dee Cohen (Prescott, AZ), poet, fiction writer, photographer, poetry columnist, and Southwest resident, is the author of *Lime Avenue Evening*, a poetry chapbook. Her work has been published in various journals, books, and newspapers. Her story "By Heart" was selected for inclusion in *The Best Small Fictions 2015*. She writes a poetry column for *5enses Magazine*.
deecohen.com

On a Clear Day

Jack Granath

An actually rectangular cloud above a pink (not pinkish) mountain, in the foreground a narrow band of terracotta stubbled with dark and dusty greens, all set against a dizzying, impossible plane of blue like no other blue in the skies of this world. So Georgia got it right, and her art, a little disappointingly, makes sense. The tourists lunge around with their camera phones capturing the corners of ersatz adobe buildings against that sky. Georgia got it right. She came here, and she did that, and no one can take it away.

A little later, though, on the train through Las Vegas (not Nevada): crooked trailers with piles of junk in the yard and ruins of carports leaning in a litter of more junk and junkyard dogs on gray ropes, propane tanks and two human figures just sitting on a railroad tie or a log. But maybe Georgia got that right too, the bones.

Hearing the word again, the old man winces. He never noticed. Ninety times a day at fairs like these, he must have heard it breathed, the watchword used by those who do not come to purchase but who wish to give a sign that, with respect, they will be moving on to hang their faces over someone else's art. He hears it—*lovely!*—and despairs.

Jack Granath (Shawnee, KS). Biographical note, page 80.

Turquoise

Vince Puzick

The hospice nurse checked the morphine drip and measured my mother's vitals, then dabbed and dribbled water from a sponge onto Mom's lips and tongue. The nurse's turquoise necklace dangled as she leaned over my mother's bed.

Some say turquoise calms and soothes. Some say the stones allow one to release negative energies, to clear the throat, to increase connection and communication.

My mother always loved turquoise. The trip to Taos some thirty years before this night remains a favorite childhood memory. My mother returned home with necklaces of blue-green stones laid in elaborately smithed silver.

Now, my mother reached to touch the nurse's necklace. The nurse leaned in, mindful, intentional, as if this were the most important moment, for as long as my mother needed.

> drying fingers touched each polished stone,
> like prayer beads, a rosary,
> bridging the earthly with the heavenly,
>
> touch as light as the sound of aspen leaves
> falling in autumn,
>
> quiet as a whispered prayer

Under a vague light from the corner, my mother spoke into the room, into the distance. Breathy, yet with what I now think was veiled anticipation, with relief, she said, *Well, is that Uncle Paul?*

I laughed nervously, reflexively, and said, *No, Mom.* She may have furrowed her brow at my intrusive voice. She wasn't talking to us.

My sister whispered, *Shh. It could definitely be Uncle Paul.*

My mother stood at the threshold. Who knew who would greet her?

What Goes Before

Mark Jodon

Just a short walk down a low hill into the arroyo leads to the opening of the narrow slot canyon. A sign warns of mountain lions and what to do if one is encountered—do not run; slowly back away; try to look as big as possible; pick up your children; fight back if attacked. Inside the canyon, the towering walls serve as trail guide, narrowing, descending to the closed end where the Rio Grande can be heard but not seen. Closed canyons, like sacred labyrinths, are walked for different reasons. What you see along the way depends.... Today, upon returning to the entrance, there in the sand, fresh paw prints enter the mouth of the canyon and then, suddenly, turn back without explanation.

Vince Puzick (Colorado Springs, CO) focuses on themes of family, nature, education, and recovery. He has had pieces published in *River Teeth Journal, Rougarou Journal of Arts & Literature, The Dewdrop,* and *On The Seawall.* When he is not at his writing table, Vince may be found fly fishing on one of Colorado's rivers or streams. He lives with his wife, daughter, two step-daughters, and many pets in Colorado.

Mark Jodon (Houston, TX). Biographical note, page 13.

Boom Town: West Texas Memories

Priscilla Frake

1981

Heat is a charlatan preacher, thumping and pounding from the sky's pulpit. Praise the Lord. Praise the Lord. Come Jesus Christ, descend into these silhouettes shaken out of darkness: a burning cross, a football player's splinted pain, a school kid in a new Camaro. Friday night. Amen. Amen.

Everything backwards: Water is salt. Wind is sand. Air is weight, too hot to breathe. Pump jacks pull up mansions from the dirt. Pictures wash in molten light to empty flatness, glitzy houses, rubbery mesquite. A shiny new mall stands up against the skyline like a movie set. Alleluia. Alleluia.

Behind the tracks, a coffee shop: red-checked tablecloths shiny with grease, raw insulation on the ceiling, scattered shacks and rusty pickups. Praise the Lord. A cowboy town of blank suburbs and air-conditioned banks, windows blazing as day scabs over. Washed in the blood of the Lamb. A sunset the color of cauterized meat dissolves into deepest blues.

Priscilla Frake (Asheville, NC) is the author of *Correspondence*, a book of epistolary poems. She has work in *Verse Daily, Nimrod, The Midwest Quarterly, Medical Literary Messenger, Carbon Culture Review, Spoon River Poetry Review,* and *The New Welsh Review,* among others. Anthology publications include *Weaving the Terrain: 100 Word Southwestern Poems, Enchantment of the Ordinary,* and *Women. Period.* Her honors include the Lorene Pouncey Award at the Houston Poetry Festival and a Pushcart nomination.

Communion

Catherine Strisik

Damp pages curl up from the outside rain like the fist of the ecclesiastical priest who spews *holy holy* from tight lips onto my neck with the precision of a bullseye. The shadow lies confused. All his power evident in his pounding. *Do I continue to eat God?* I expose my shoulders only. Though I swim the Grande's edge. The breast stroke and when I open my eyes the water snakes and female ducks tremble. I look and don't look dangerous. And afraid. I like distance between myself and my beauty. *I feel like eating God.* I am not hungry. I am not ordinary. The rain spills into my want mouth. My body and my holy extravagant. The priest cloaked in moss and fern. The puzzle trees. *Already tasting me everywhere and my hands, too.* You continue to lick the salt block. I approach *imperfect and preferred.* Without clothes in torn Nikes.

Catherine Strisik (Taos, NM), Taos Poet Laureate, 2020–21, is the author of *Insectum Gravitis* and *The Mistress*, respectively winner and finalist for the New Mexico–Arizona Book Award (2017 and 2020). Recipient of the 2020 Taoseña Award as Woman of Impact based on literary contributions, Catherine is editor and co-founder of *Taos Journal of Poetry*. Her poetry has been translated into Greek, Persian, and Bulgarian. cathystrisik.com

Dawn in Raton

Alan Birkelbach

He noticed the browned and bent curves of the single leaf from the peach tree as it trembled on the ground from its falling. He waited, *one two three,* then the wind stroked it and offered the other side, veined and freckled, yellow, a blush of pink. Sitting in the rocking chair his father had made, he was left having to decide which side of the leaf he loved the most. What about the cheekbones and quivering lips he had—just a few minutes ago—left behind on the pillow?

He'd moved here for the silence. The mesa, across town, seemed ancient, wise, and still enough. He realized it was probably conspiring, along with the wind, which was, even now, carrying away the steam from his coffee. He thought, sardonically, that maybe a timeless, bound ghost of himself down south might yet need that awakening.

Awakening was such a good word. Just to the southeast he could see the volcanic plain, the sleeping cones, dormant for thousands of years. Behind his house, within blocks, was the iridium layer, the black geologic evidence of the meteor that had crashed into the gulf. But everything here, now, was sleeping—mesa, volcanoes, iridium layer.

He had been told that solitude amplified creativity, but he wasn't yet sure. Sometimes, it was all he could do to count breaths. In the spaces between inhales and exhales, he realized that he had, in the other life, not paid attention to quiet. He couldn't remember any years of wind, leaves, the imagining of far-off rumbling.

He rose from the rocker. The leaf had been carried down the block. The hunger for solitude was not a sin. He knew that much. There was more than enough quiet to heal him.

He was in love with both sides of the leaf, both sides of the sleeping face. He would crawl back beneath the covers. Maybe she would turn her head. The tremor of dawn would catch her sleeping smile.

Boot Library

karla k. morton

Double Take Resale, Santa Fe, NM

Come to the classics when you're lonely, your belly full, your bladder empty; twelve quarters for the parking meter. *You are going to be here a while.* Start downstairs in the Western Room, feel giddy in the hushed rush of the stacks, hundreds of cowboy boots bursting into view, lined up on shelves in Dewey-Decimal sizing; biographical books, each: right toe out, left toe in, for full volume viewing. Pure periodical art: colors, lettering, tooling, stitching, by some old man who worked his whole life in bovine-bound soles, with hide thick enough for snake bite. It is encyclopedic non-fiction, rows of poetry, history—its own unique genre.

In the carrel, I try on a pair that begins to crumble, desperate for bindery, age finally turning cowhide back to dust—a soft language reclaimed in the lips of the earth. I come when I'm lonely, these books of boots, paisanos thirsting for the oils of human touch, the hook of stirrup, the legacy of the next generation—passed forward hand to hand, foot to leathered foot.

I buy the red boots, bundle them home, wonder what cowgirl spirit is still waltzing within them as they yield to my feet— whose ankles they wrapped, what color stallion they flanked as she leaned forward in the saddle, whispering sweet and sugar in his ear.

Alan Birkelbach (Raton, NM). Biographical note, page 6.

---

karla k. morton (Raton, NM). Biographical note, page 18.

Boot Scoot Nights

Claire Vogel Camargo

Come evening time, folks head out for some boot scootin' fun. Couples two-step, circling the dance floor en masse to country-western music. As the Cotton-Eyed Joe starts up, dancers form lines like spokes in a wheel, stepping and turning as one.

> side-by-side
> with strangers
> grapevining

Others lean against the bar or sit at tables around the dance floor, listening to country stars sing, or talking and drinking. From all walks of life and ages. Many dressed in jeans and boots or skirts and boots, and Stetsons. Amidst laughter and whistles, eyes rove and may meet. Smiles flash. Some people go to the dancehall just to dance. Maybe a few are searching for someone to leave with. Perhaps there is hope of finding *the one.*

> lookin' for happy
> where most songs are sad
> mistaken signals

Claire Vogel Camargo (Austin, TX) jumped into haibun in 2017, won a 2018 Sakura Award in the Vancouver Cherry Blossom Haiku Festival, placed or received honorable mentions in other contests, including tenth and fourteenth Yamadera Bashō Memorial Museum English Haiku Contests. Her work has been selected for inclusion in *skipping stones: The Red Moon Anthology of English-Language Haiku 2022*. A Touchstone Award 2020 Nominee and published haiku poet, Claire also writes free verse. She authored *Iris Opening* (2017).

An Ear for Music

Gustavo Adolfo Aybar

So, come on, let it go. Just let it be.
Why don't you be you and I'll be me?
Everything that's broke, leave it to the breeze.
Let the ashes fall; forget about me.
James Bay, "Let It Go"

My son sings the song as if he's listened to it since birth. He's five. It'll take four more years before I realize he has an aptitude for remembering musical sounds and melodies. The staccato bass rifts of our merengue. The spiraling guitar lines in our bachata, and the ukulele-infused ballad his mother and I listen to in our separate homes. Separate vehicles. A break-up song. Because he wishes to attend public school in this country, he must also learn to recognize the sound of high velocity rounds. To distinguish firecracker from bullet. Sidearm from shotgun. A hostile from a friendly individual. Because he's Latino and his home was broken, they'll think his body deserves to be broken. He says, *Mami listens to it too*, and cries, *Papi, you just sing.*

Gustavo Adolfo Aybar (Kansas City, MO) is a Dominican poet whose early years in Los Angeles shaped much of what he loves: baseball and the Dodgers, Magic and the Lakers. His first collection, *We Seek Asylum,* captures his struggle to be at once a critic of his island and the sport, and a lover of his culture. Gustavo is working on a travelogue/black belt journey collection of stories related to being a single father and a martial artist.

Singular

Eleanor Kedney

The dog and I walk early before townhome lights turn on and buzz saws derail birdsong. I linger over rainwater pin drops in spider silk and a creosote's smoky spice. Between facing units, agaves formed spirals, and the hunched-back roots of the desert willow long ago broke hard ground. It's a mind settling moment—a wick dipper—when memories hold vigil, their flame burning through 3 a.m. sleep. A dove collides with a window and flies beyond. Another hits wind chimes on a neighbor's porch—a terrible tremble—the bird on its back, beak parted, legs upturned. Stunned, I rush the dog home, return with a shoebox and cardboard for scooping, but the bird has righted itself beneath a table. In dark shadow, calm. Hour after hour, I check on it. Its head turns slightly toward me. I visited my mother in the hospital twice a day for a month, her monitored heart with flat mesas and unclimbable peaks—meaningless. Her eyes' stillness. Her exhales numbered. She forgot where she lived. The last visit was the last. The dove gone.

Eleanor Kedney (Tucson, AZ) is the author of *Between the Earth and Sky* (C&R Press, 2020), a finalist for the 2021 New Mexico–Arizona Book Award and the 2020 Best Book Award. Her chapbook is *The Offering* (Liquid Light Press, 2016). Eleanor is the founder of the Tucson branch of the New York-based Writers Studio; she served as the director for ten years. She joined the board of the Tucson Poetry Festival in 2021. eleanorkedney.com.

Impulse to Serve

Stan Crawford

Our brown tangle-haired terrier barks to warn us about threats only he can hear and no one can see. He stands at our front door, chest thrown out, eyes blazing, howling his alarm. Outside, nothing but an empty street and the impassive faces of the Sandias. No UPS, no FedEx, no Amazon—none of his traditional enemies. Not even a bird in the almond tree in our front yard, its leaves barely moving in the silent air. Not a single roadrunner skipping through the dust. Inside, warnings of chaos, Götterdämmerung. His eyes roll back in his head like a backwoods evangelist handling a rattlesnake.

> sabotaged by fury
> pain of consciousness,
> Buddhists say

Stan Crawford (Albuquerque, NM) lives with his wife Dawn and their assorted pets, including Jake, the terrier featured in "Impulse to Serve." Stan's poems have been published in *Borderlands: Texas Poetry Review, The Comstock Review, The Midwest Quarterly, The Ocotillo Review, Poet Lore, Water-Stone Review,* and elsewhere. His poetry collection *Resisting Gravity* (Lamar University Literary Press) was a finalist for Best First Book of Poetry from the Texas Institute of Letters in 2017.

Postcard from the Nevada Proving Ground

Morgan Ray

They gave it such a fun name—*Operation Buster-Jangle,* offered free front-row foxholes and fashion sunglasses to our troops so they could watch the blast up close. They even built a furnished house for a family of life-size dolls to see if they'd implode. Ranchers described the cloud as a *terrible beauty,* said an eerie ash fell on nearby lands where cows were grazing on sage. Some reported snow that glowed an iridescent blue. The authorities said it was completely safe, no need to fear prevailing winds, no need to fret about fallout making its way into cartons of milk.

Morgan Ray (Salt Lake City, UT). Biographical note, page 72.

Chimayó

Miriam Sagan

The oncologist told me that if the lit-up area the PET scan showed on my pancreas was a tumor, the cancer would be incurable.

Since I don't plan to treat much in any case, I asked my question. If a second tumor, life expectancy without treatments is one year. If just a breast tumor, one to two years. It is kind of daunting to have to live, but intriguing. *How to—* that's my next question.

Went to the Santuario de Chimayó. It is a healing shrine, Catholic, although sometimes it feels older than that. It has a church, altars, and a pit of healing dirt. Isn't that what northern New Mexicans are supposed to do with a bad diagnosis? There was snow on the mountains, yellow foliage, pouring rain, and thick fog on the high road. I sat in the chapel and touched the healing dirt. I touched it to my breast. I put money in the box and looked at the bank of candles. Outside, catalpa trees and running streams.

> wet petals
> on late roses—
> a wall of crutches

Miriam Sagan (Santa Fe, NM). Biographical note, page 46.

While I'm Thinking of Lascaux

Laurie Wilcox-Meyer

and her landline dangling from a telephone pole, my neighbor digs into clay and rock. One day her body will be placed in this grave. She ferments cabbage and peppers. Foraging for osha root, she honors the rattlesnakes. Desert sage and yucca beyond the arroyo. Her footprint is barely there.

> echoes in a cave
> my greater fear …
> cardiogram

Laurie Wilcox-Meyer (Asheville, NC). Biographical note, page 19.

Waiting for the Sun

Janet Ruth

My body, my senses have fallen for New Mexico—fire of green chile—earth of tamales—spice of sandsage after rain—curve-billed thrasher's serenade—an incendiary sunrise above the Sandías—autumn's crisp, cool air after summer's heat.

But, here in the desert, a secret longing—for a place far to the east, a time far in my past.

> saltgrass waves
> wash over young dreams
> waiting for high tide

My body, my senses, harbor a hidden yearning. For regular susurrations of waves drowned out by laughing gulls' recriminations. Smells of salt, algae, and dead sea creatures lifting from jetsam laid in a twisted ribbon at high tide line. Greasy, salty flesh of boardwalk fries, saltwater taffy's tooth-binding sweetness. Lifted to the Atlantic's surface—the sun's orange globe. Smooth ocean—with strands of pelicans, a stitch of dolphins. Empty beach, but for sanderlings chasing waves in and out. And my toes—oh, my toes dream of being unbound. Splayed in sand—no worries about cholla spines—flexed in search of nothing more dangerous than a rough sand dollar or intact slipper shell.

> sands still fresh with salt
> vie with those from ancient seas
> my gritty heart

Janet Ruth (Corrales, NM). Biographical note, page 40.

Hands

Janice Whittington

How unimaginative my fingers, the claws they have become, so unlike the sharp talons of the kestrel, small in its bloody grasping. Age grabs my hands in its clutches, a red-tailed hawk gripping. The veins stand like those sentinels at my father's grave, all blue and military. At night, I look up to stars far away in the ether, and I cannot see my hands in the dark. I want to take pen and write until dawn when the light returns with my dappled skin. No owls cough up my fur after the night's hunt, no other hand reaches for mine, all bone and memory.

Janice Whittington (Lubbock, TX) has previously published the collection *Into a Thousand Mouths,* a Walt McDonald Series Winner from Texas Tech University Press. She has a poetry chapbook, *Does My Father Dream of Sons?* (University of West Florida). Her poems have appeared in various journals as well. Janice admits that nature slips into all of her writing, as she is surrounded with the dust, wide spaces, creatures, and beauty of all that is around her.

Shelley Armitage (Las Cruces, NM), a member of the Texas Institute of Letters, held the Roderick Professorship at the University of Texas–El Paso. She is author of eight award-winning books, most recently *Walking the Llano: A Texas Memoir of Place,* a *Kirkus Review* starred book cited as one of the best memoirs of the year and a finalist for the May Sarton Prize, the New Mexico–Arizona Book Award, and the Collins P. Carr Book Award. *A Habit of Landscape* (Finishing Line Press) is Shelley's forthcoming poetry collection.
shelleyarmitage.com

Removal

Shelley Armitage

No wonder I hunkered down in your gardening shed that day, the day of your funeral, comforted by shovels, clumps of dirt dried fast, your calico bonnet hanging near. Without you, I turn to chemicals: the wart on my hand slowly disappears, nothing like waking one morning to find it—and your healing touch—gone. What was it Mother said? That the secret is passed from mother to daughter like a prayer. I believed. I believed. I believed in you. The secret came from your grandmother, just sepia now, aging as the only photograph of her does, marked on the back *Grandma Long* (whose handwriting?)—clearly someone more than just the wife of a Methodist circuit rider. Was he home much, that traveling man, the one who changed her name, removed her with his history still safe within the family, a tiny weathered Psalm book, his name permanently inscribed, the saddlebag's snug fit. *Abide with me.* Her name I couldn't find no matter what circuits I searched, what rolls, what records I checked: North Carolina, Oklahoma, southern Illinois, Texas. One of the lost ones, she disappeared yet seems sternly present in her Western dress, tight lace collar, prim buttons, deep-set eyes a spark against skin the color of the dirt floor in her granddaughter's backyard shed. And you, grandmother, whose hands healed wounds— the green thumb, the herbalist's touch—I last saw through the steam of a local cleaners where in the back room you pressed wrinkles from some stranger's long pants. The secret was to be passed from mother to daughter. A prayer, a prayer. Though adopted, I long to hear the whisper in the blood.

Salt Plains Moon

Margaret Dornaus

It's cold and dark when I pull up to the Sunny Lane rambler Aunt Ruth has called home for as long as I can remember. She's asked to join me on the two-and-a-half-hour drive north from Midwest City to Oklahoma's Salt Plains. To see the snow geese. I honk my horn and settle in to wait for my aunt's appearance. Soon enough, she's setting a large thermos of coffee between us. She says she can't remember the last time she had a real adventure.

> the road ahead …
> an endless ribbon of silk
> trailing moonlight

I've heard the best chance for a sighting is daybreak when, roused from sleep, the snow geese take off in wave after wave of ribboned hunting parties. But somewhere between shared cups of coffee and chitchat, time's taken the moon hostage. I try to cover my disappointment as we watch the sun rise above the Salt Plains, but Aunt Ruth can't hold back. *We've missed them!* she cries. Still, when she reaches for my hand, my heart skips a beat. And then another.

Native Oklahoman **Margaret Dornaus** (Ozark, AR) employs a variety of forms—from haibun and tanka prose to free verse narratives—in her poetry. A Pushcart Prize and Best of the Net nominee, Margaret has work in numerous journals and anthologies, including *I-70 Review, One Art,* and *Red Earth Review.* Her book *Prayer for the Dead: Collected Haibun & Tanka Prose* (Singing Moon Press, 2016) tied for second place in the 2017 Haiku Society of America's Mildred Kanterman Book Awards.

WINTER

Obscurity

Marilyn Westfall

Overnight, a soft, heavy snow erased the land we came to hike in northern Arizona, shaped by over a billion years of uplift, rockslide, erosion by water and wind. Even the prized vermilion layer, like dusk dyed into quartz, a tourist attraction, was blanched—without pause of white accumulation. Our boots left deep imprints as, bare-handed, we scraped door handles, slipped inside, coaxed the engine to start and ran the defroster while a norther wailed and shook our rental Jeep.

> Aeolian wind
> shaper of hills and deserts
> we sit in its grip

Marilyn Westfall (Lubbock, TX) earned a PhD in Creative Writing and Literature from Texas Tech University in Lubbock, where she chairs the longstanding Ad Hoc Writers group—and is fortunate to do so. Her poems appear in earlier Dos Gatos Press anthologies, as well as in *The Southern Poetry Anthology, Volume VIII: Texas.* Recent poems are included in *Evening Street Review, Sand Hills Literary Magazine, Dream Noir, Big Bend Literary Magazine, Duality,* and *One Sentence Poems.*

Carta para mi Patrimonio

Evaleah Caceres

On faithless nights, México comes to mind. She is green, but She is ancient. La luz de un gran arrobamiento se acerca, más acerca, con los vientos del invierno, y solo tengo que mirar a la luna y adoro para vivir sin cesar. Mi papá es un hijo de México, pero también he is of Italy, and he is of Spain, so I am weary of watching la luna y adorando y ser preguntando: *What is it to come from both the killers and their prey?* Los conquistadores y los sacrificados run in my blood with México. I sit in the rare snowfall, la nevada delicada, of the Mojave desert, and I remember when I did not know who I was. I watch the moon, and I worship, and I wonder: *Do I get to hold this heritage, when I did not always know it was mine?* The daughters of México surround me, all holding hands, and they remind me of when people would ask *what are you?—¿Eres una Chicana?*—and I would answer *no*, because I did not know those daughters' hands were mine to hold. I try to stand alongside them now, surrounding myself. I am Dante, on a pilgrimage, siempre y siempre, por mi identidad. Él buscó al Paraíso; yo estoy buscando a México. She is ancient, but She is ever-changing; I am una hija de Ella, and I think that means I am allowed to change too.

Translations:

La luz de un gran arrobamiento.... *The light of a great rapture grows close, and closer, with the winter winds, and all I have to do to live forever is watch the moon and worship.*

Mi papá es un hijo.... *My father is a son of Mexico, but he is also of Italy, and he is of Spain, so I am weary of watching the moon, and worshipping, and wondering:*

Los conquistadores y los sacrificados: *The conquerors and the sacrificed*

la nevada delicada: *the fragile snowfall*

siempre y siempre, por mi identidad.... *ever and ever, for my identity. He looked for heaven; I look for Mexico.*

una hija de Ella: *one of her daughters*

In the Mimbres Valley

Miriam Sagan

I tire of walking in the snowy arroyo, following footprints left by God knows who. My mood deteriorates. Leaning on my cane I follow you, not wanting to disappoint your faith in my enthusiasm. Suddenly, I come upon a huge boulder completely covered in swirling marine fossils—the jellyfish and sea cucumbers of the pre-Cambrian seas, invertebrate swirls like stone whirlpools. And someone, greedy and eager, has chiseled off a substantial chunk. I judge them, these unseen thieves, but can't blame them completely.

> in my change purse
> tiny red chip of
> an ancient pot

Just five more minutes, you say. But I've given up and am sitting on a rock, sobbing with pain and effort. I've cursed you, the snow, my feet inappropriately in sneakers, my lame right leg, my stubborn pride. And you have a cellphone snap to show me—the unexciting sketchy pictograph you were in search of. It isn't dramatic, but you have the satisfaction of a quest fulfilled.

Walking back, I'm glad I gave up when I did. My eyes on the ground, I see more fossils.

> chock full of tiny
> shimmering crystals
> black volcanic rock

Evaleah Caceres (Las Vegas, NV), a high school student, writes poetry and plays; she is currently working on her first novel. Her play *Dollface* was produced at Las Vegas Academy of the Arts as part of the Academy's annual New Works Festival, and she wrote several short pieces for the 2022 Theatre III showcase, *At Sixes and Sevens*.
Instagram: @tobeornot_whataquestion

Miriam Sagan (Santa Fe, NM). Biographical note, page 46.

Chaco Canyon Pilgrimage

Goyo

Canyon winds sigh. They sigh against these high wailing walls that lean into New Mexico's cobalt-blue winter sky. Sediments of shale and sand and mud lay down around the periphery of sixty-six-million-year-old cretaceous seas to become walls that recall prehistory. Each hand-placed sandstone, like a tongue, sings the solstice to the ancient ones, a chorus that echoes forward to present-day pilgrims. At dusk the walls chant in November light that paints the east wall of Chaco Canyon in blood.

The canyon tells her own story: carved by Chaco Wash over millenia since Chicxulub fell out of the sky, dinosaurs fell to their knees to become mineralized supplicants frozen into layered Morrison sandstone. The frog petroglyph—pecked higher than the reach of human hands into Cliff House sandstone—crawls farther up on its powerful talons, croaks at the now distant sea. I have ears. I listen: for the ringing buzz of the rock wren as it hops on and around cracked-off talus boulders, calls among the rock jumble like a fishing-reel drag, set high, yanked out fast.

In late afternoon, winds die. The air fills with sunlit dust motes. The raucous loggerhead shrike—perched in the dull green, four-wing salt bush—quiets behind its dark mask.

Breathing heavily, my unslaked throat and dry mouth are hushed as I clamber up the west canyon wall towards the pueblo ruin Tsin Kletsin, silhouetted by an orange sun lowering itself through West Gap. At my back, a solitary raven rides an updraft. A black cloud whisp drifts over the canyon. Thunder cracks. Coiled lightning strikes the canyon rim.

Goyo (Albuquerque, NM). Biographical note, page 9.

Topaz at Night

Rita Ciresi

Stars like spilled glitter. Tumbleweeds in the wind. Through the shattered glass of the barracks pokes a thin face—ghost of Nikkei who lived here, who died, who wished he'd never been born? He tilts his head back and howls, this lonely coyote.

Rita Ciresi (Tampa, FL) is author of the novels *Bring Back My Body to Me, Pink Slip, Blue Italian,* and *Remind Me Again Why I Married You;* the story collections *Sometimes I Dream in Italian* and *Mother Rocket;* and two award-winning collections of flash fiction, *Female Education* and *Second Wife.*

Editor's Note: The Topaz War Relocation Center—also called the Central Utah Relocation Center—was a United States concentration camp that incarcerated citizens or resident immigrants of Japanese descent during the Second World War.

The Last Conquistador

Kathryn Jones

The piñon pines saw who did it … an amputation without anesthesia … a severing without screams.

Rebellion, reckoning, revenge. An eye for an eye, a foot for a foot. The bronze-booted right foot of conquistador Don Juan de Oñate, sawed off one December night two dozen years ago in tiny Alcalde, New Mexico. He ordered prisoners' toes—some accounts say entire feet—cut off so they could not escape. Should he not suffer the same fate symbolically?

The conquistador's eyes showed no fear or pain as he stared into the sky atop his horse. Old ghosts urged on the avenger: *Saw, saw, saw!* Black crows danced and sang: *Caw, caw, caw!* Oñate's left foot survived, painted red with the words *Remember 1680*, year of the Pueblo revolt when, at Acoma, the people tossed Spaniards over cliffs. Revolution … such bloody business.

The avenger hid the booted foot like a treasure, a treasure with no value except to others who knew. Newspapers wrote stories asking who, who, who could do such a deed? Others smiled. Vengeance … bloodless but nonetheless sweet.

The legacy of conquest runs long, deep, red. Old resentments simmer like bitter broth over embers of revolt never extinguished. Oñate's statue on horseback, new foot welded on, looks whole again. Invisible cracks run beneath the bronze patina. The piñon trees know. The crows know. He did not conquer anyone.

Languages Lost

Shelley Armitage

Adopted basalt, repatinated creosote, scratching down the already evicted image from some past gradually dissolved. High above on igneous escarpments jagged walls of kindred spirits. Light skips by moments in time now present. Ozymandias in our desert. Plumed serpent, goggle-eyed, quiet of soul. Risen pentimento, solace-chipped twilight of culture, undulating lines of vectored diamonds. Why these petroglyphs, X-rays won't tell. You and I know only A:shiwi will.

Kathryn Jones (Walnut Springs, TX) has poetry in literary journals and anthologies, including *Odes and Elegies: Eco-Poetry from the Texas Gulf Coast* (Lamar University Literary Press, 2021) and *Lone Star Poetry* (Kallisto Gaia Press, 2022). A longtime journalist, Kathryn has written for numerous magazines and newspapers, including *The New York Times* and *Texas Monthly.* Her essays have been published in books about film, literature, and songwriting. Kathryn is a member of the Texas Institute of Letters.

Shelley Armitage (Las Cruces, NM). Biographical note, page 106.

César Chávez, We Are Here To Help

Ellen Sazzman

1974, Calexico, California District Office,
United Farm Workers of America

We five UC Berkeley law students arrive in Calexico to organize lettuce pickers in the Imperial Valley. Given that *no hablamos Español*, God only knows what we're doing—aside from reviewing union membership rolls—when a very pregnant lady waddles in, talking rapidly in Spanish. She winces and points to her belly. Not until the director returns in ten, do we understand she wants directions to the nearest hospital so her baby will be born an American citizen.

People flow across the bridge between the two sun-beaten towns of Mexicali and Calexico—no patrols or fences—like the Rio Nuevo's free run with no consideration of residency, Spanish heard more frequently than English. Stalls of street fare and handicrafts stretch skin to skin over the road's softening lip and a fontanel of shifting plates. Back then, birth was a hypothetical threat to be avoided with barriers and pills, and borders were supposedly poured in cement and engraved on official documents.

After four days, I take the bus from Calexico to Barstow, admiring the Salton Sea's barrenness, its salt-encrusted basin balanced on a fault. I meet up with friends and share my newfound wisdom: borders are meaningless divisions set by racist politicians. We all sleep in the barn, someone's parents' chicken farm, and sample kinds of sex. It's my first time, in my defense, that I drink margaritas, three of them. The salt on the rim is addictive.

It takes ten more years to learn births are no theoretical fancy but bloody messes that hurt like hell no matter how deep the *pant pant puff,* or what language the swearing. I trace the jagged scar of my C-section, where sutures bind north and south together. And feel convulsions along my belly.

Reading Rooms

M.C. Childs

Zimmerman Library, Albuquerque

John Gaw Meem inked plans and details for six-foot thick walls, high ceilings, tall windows, good light. Wilma Loy Shelton turned the first shovelful of earth on December 2, 1936. Faustin Talachi, Daniel Mirabel, and Justin Yassie carved spirits of animals and tempers of weather deep into long *vigas*. Abad Eloy Lucero hand-hewed oak tables and chairs. Walter B. Gilbert crafted chandeliers of punched tin, wrought iron, etched glass, and mirrors. Craftsmen erected steel; placed peeled aspen *savinos* between *vigas*; bent wrought-iron gates, banisters, and door handles; and carved steam-heat register guards from New Mexican pine. When they were done, the parade lasted for two weeks; the brass band played; in coats and ties, dresses and heels, students, faculty, and WPA workers ferried books to the new library.

> silent students
> read, write, hold hands
> study echoes

Ellen Sazzman (Potomac, MD), a Pushcart-nominated poet, has recent work in *Peregrine, Delmarva Review, Another Chicago Magazine, PANK, Ekphrastic Review, Sow's Ear,* and *Common Ground,* among others. Ellen received an honorable mention in the Ginsberg contest and was shortlisted for the O'Donoghue Prize. Her collection *The Shomer* was selected as a finalist for the 2020 Blue Lynx Prize and a semifinalist for the 2020 Elixir Antivenom Award and the 2019 Codhill Press Award.

M.C. Childs (Seattle, WA). Biographical note, page 38.

Lord, It Was Different Then

Ken Wheatcroft-Pardue

a story my grandmother once told me

When was it? '46, maybe '47? Anyway, after the war cause it wasn't so hard to get gas and tires worth a damn. Before interstates, we had to poke through one Podunk town after another. Once, a roadblock stopped us. Ahead a tanker carrying gas had jack-knifed, flipped, exploded. All they could do was let it flame out. So the highway closed, and we just sat there. Then up came a blue norther. Whirly winds of red dust funneled right past our windshield while a whole line of smudge pots blew out one by one. And we just shivered in that old Nash. We were so damn cold. Then my Tom remembered the flask in the glove compartment. We took a few draws, and I tell you, it sure warmed up our insides. Lord, it was different then. About then, a rancher drove up, cut some barbed wire, led all the waiting cars through a field. As we drove, we could see those flames shooting up thirty, forty feet in the air, like an inferno, casting huge shadows of those old tank-like cars, their shocks bobbing in the rutty pastures that weren't no more a road than a dirt path. The rancher cut some more barbed wire, waved us all on back to the road. Sometimes my Tom could sure be a smart ass. When we passed the rancher, he tipped his flask at him. After all these years, I still see that rancher shaking his bent finger at us, like we was up to no good, but he had a nice grin when he done it, so we knew it was really all the same to him. Lord, it was different then.

Retired high school teacher **Ken Wheatcroft-Pardue** (Fort Worth, TX) is the author of a recent poetry collection, *What I Did Not Tell You* (Hungry Buzzard Press, 2020). Ken is an essayist, sometime journalist, and short story writer. He has published more than a hundred poems in such venues as *The Texas Observer, Red River Review, California Quarterly, Concho River Review, Borderlands,* two anthologies of Texas poetry, and numerous other publications.

Trading Post

Sandi Stromberg

As though nails and planks can scab their wounds, the disheartened couple board up the failed general store and scuttle away like scorpions. A dozen grackles watch, then chatter as they pick through rubbish tangled in gray-green saltbrush. Locked inside, dreams suffocate in blackstrap molasses. They hide under the tongues of the till, the forgotten one-dollar bills.

>tin cans corroding
>leak unnamable contents
>mouse droppings still soft

A grandson crowbars the door, then stands in the stab of sunlight slicing the darkness. He hesitates, his breath shallow in the heavy smell of dust and decay. Behind him on the sagging porch, a solitary raven watches, then cackles like an old gossip. Motes gather in the sudden glare.

>from silent corners
>whispers float toward the light
>ghosts slip out the door

Sandi Stromberg (Houston, TX) ended her nomadic life when she landed in Space City and began to write poetry instead of magazine features. Sandi has been nominated three times for a Pushcart Prize and twice for Best of the Net. Her full-length poetry collection *Frogs Don't Sing Red* is forthcoming (Kelsay Books, 2023). Widely published in small literary journals and anthologies, Sandi recently became an editor at *The Ekphrastic Review*.

After the Chainsaws Have Stopped

Cindy Huyser

I tell myself—as if I were a tour guide—*Here's the world*, a place that gives itself day after day to dark. The sun's blade settles on spindly tips of invasive bamboo, late day's faint yellow flame turning them like tinder.

But I'm the one who's brittle, who sees this outgrown grass that's pushed past asphalt as a lesson in resilience. Taller now than the creosote-soaked trees we call phone poles, dead ones spending the afterlife answering to someone else's name. Slogging burdens of light.

Maybe to notice absence is to see what's in its place. The amputation splinters into saturation, fingers pressing bruises into bark.

There's sky above the rust-brown heart.

Cindy Huyser (Austin, TX), a multiple Pushcart nominee, has poems in a variety of journals and anthologies. Her chapbook *Burning Number Five: Power Plant Poems* was co-winner of the 2014 Blue Horse Press Poetry Chapbook contest. Cindy co-edited *Bearing the Mask: Southwestern Persona Poems* (Dos Gatos Press, 2016) and several editions of the *Texas Poetry Calendar.*

Inside Out

Dee Cohen

Standing at the kitchen sink, sun barely rising, blush of light behind the trees, I rinse glasses, then glance out—it is just that much lighter, and again, that much lighter, like I've caught the sky unfolding, a curtain hitched up to reveal the Sandias expanding by moments. And then I glance out again, and you are there, making your way from the garage back to the house on the gravel path. You're an early riser now in these first careful weeks of sobriety, head down; it's hard not to count the stark days silhouetted against our lives like cranes that pass overhead, cries unfolding.

You are inside and outside, known and unknown, a familiar friend, then a stranger again. Days where your hand is an old glove I'm holding and other days where there are no hands, no gloves, just your solitary way on the gravel path. And now the sky is boldly brighter, striped with pastels, and you've paused to look in the window. Me inside, you out. *Can you see me? Yes, you can,* and your smile opens, early riser, like the light in the sky, unfolding.

Dee Cohen (Prescott, AZ). Biographical note, page 90.

Two Weeks before Christmas, Santa Fe

Katherine DiBella Seluja

Heading south on Saint Francis, I was returning from the store. A bag full of cheese and yogurt, cereal and fruit. Bottle of pinot grigio. It was already dark. Above the trees and the apartment building on our corner, an unusual grouping of lights in the sky. Five red glowing spheres, floating up. A spontaneous constellation, they maintained their distance evenly, or so it seemed, for a few moments. Until they slow-drifted apart. Allowing dark and southern stars and a small plane flying someone home to Dallas or away to Denver, to come between them. And I thought, yes, this is how it is to start out in the world. Arm's distance from each other. And then time, or stars, slowly fill the space between us. One moment basking in the red glow and the next, only a shimmering speck, not nearly as bright as the sheen of Las Tres Marias.

Katherine DiBella Seluja (Santa Fe, NM) is the author of *Gather the Night* and co-author of *We Are Meant to Carry Water.* Her third book of poetry, *Point of Entry*, is forthcoming (University of New Mexico Press, 2023). Recent work has appeared in *Cutthroat* and *FENCE*. Her poem "Elixir for Knowing When to Surrender" placed second in the Julia Peterkin Poetry contest and was nominated for a Pushcart Prize. Katherine works as a nurse practitioner in Española, New Mexico.

Author's Note: Las Tres Marias is the name used in several Latin American countries and the Philippines for the three stars of Orion's Belt.

New Mexican Clarity

Feroza Jussawalla

Even the coldest winter day brings blue sky, fragile as Murano, Chihuly—transparent, crystalline—like the stars that fall in the dark from the Geminid meteors on our winter nights. I pierce the blue sheen, grasping for clarity and belonging in my own life. I, who have come to New Mexico from the Decanni plateau and made it my home. It is a home that feels just like my home on the other plateau—dry, rocky, and yet with pillars of sand, Tent Rocks. My journey, long and winding, brings me from Persia, via India, a Zoroastrian, who worships and follows the stars like the Magi did. Tirgan, we call it: the festival of stars, when we gather bits of broken glass and crystal, shiny Taos mica, as though they were stars that had fallen from the sky. I stand on my balcony at night, looking for Perseid showers, hoping for bits of stars to fall on me, to give me the clarity of the morning sunshine. I search for Jupiter, hoping to see rings that might encircle me.

I am rooted here now. *Soy de la India, pero también de Nuevo México*—from India, but also from New Mexico. I grow like the little white daisies that spring up between the cracks in the rocks. When uprooted and transplanted to tropical climes, I wither. Petrichor turns to putrefaction.

As I stare into the New Mexican sky, I wonder if, when I am gone from the physical plane, New Mexico's paranormal hunters will find me in my white night gown on my balcony, many a summer and winter night, still searching for crystal clear clarity.

Feroza Jussawalla (Albuquerque, NM) is Professor Emerita at the University of New Mexico. She has been writing all her life, either scholarly work or creative pieces. Though Feroza has been doing writing practice with Natalie Goldberg since 1999, with many, many notebooks of daily writing, the bulk of her writing has been scholarly books on literatures, written in English, from various parts of the world, such as India, Africa, or the Caribbean.

A New Love Found

Bethany Jarmul

At midnight, in a desert place, a coyote howls a song about his lost lover. He howls and the cacti shiver, their blossoms shriveling, clinging one to another. He howls and the tortoises withdraw into their shells. He howls and the scorpions climb out and dance to the sound of the rattlesnakes' maracas and seductive hisses. I must decide if I will hide my tear-stained face, bury it in the cooling red sand, or raise it high and slow dance with the moonlight—a new love found.

Bethany Jarmul (Gibsonia, PA) is a writer, editor, and poet. Her work has appeared in numerous literary magazines, with nominations for Best of the Net and Best Spiritual Literature. Bethany earned first place in Women On Writing's Q2 2022 essay contest. She enjoys chai lattes, nature walks, and memoirs. She lives near Pittsburgh with her family.
bethanyjarmul.com
Twitter: @BethanyJarmul

Prescription for Widowhood

for Nancy

Sandi Stromberg

Fly to Santa Fe. Find Venus in the sky of a waxing moon. Give up maps and being *one who must know*. Your pathway is under construction in this city of red and green chiles, clanging cathedral bells, clay pots. Meditate when melatonin and the generous jigger of tequila doesn't erase the loss of your beloved.

Hold a pot in your hands. Caress its earthy roundness, its circle of life and love. Be with it. It came out of fire, strong, alive. It deserves respect. Recognize the stories of its people, separated, displaced, broken as you have been.

Place your ear on the mouth of the pot. It once held water, gray grains of salt, essences of a pueblo. It will whisper stories about the four phases of life in languages ancient as its gods. Gather the words in Tiwa, Tewa, Towa, Diné. Your heart will understand each one.

When the winter solstice comes, ground yourself in clay. Bless your cracks, your breaks, your knocks, your rough edges. Sing into yourself. Hear a song of endurance singing back.

Sandi Stromberg (Houston, TX). Biographical note, page 121.

The Poetry in Prose

Lucy's Mexican Bakery

Diana L. Conces

Last-minute Christmas gift questing for tres leches for a homesick friend, we open the door. Bells tinkle merrily along the empty mid-afternoon sidewalk past the same-day cleaners and the hair salon—and it hits us, in a one-two punch of smell and sight. Hidden ovens thicken the air—sugar, milk, flour, lard, cinnamon, and molasses—dough rising, baking. We have to breathe, breathe in, resolve cracking like the tops of the conchas, piled on their trays. Glass case on the left has tres leches, but our eyes and feet take us to the display cases and our hands find a tray to fill. Gallant puerquitos call to me, their snouts upturned, round bellies shiny with glaze. The tease of pineapple peeks out of a roll of pan dulce, entices her. Galletas of all kinds, tri-colored banderas, and the delicate folds of the orejas lie in neat stacks, while pink, coconut-dusted besos and sugar-dusted gallinas flaunt their frill of filling in exuberant piles. Tray piled high, we head to the cash register, add that square of tres leches we came for all those smells ago.

Unknotting the Line

Diana L. Conces (Round Rock, TX). Biographical note, page 38.

Sun-Baked Terra Cotta

Tricia Knoll

I need a Christmas gift. For my retired man who says he has everything as he approaches his eighty-ninth birthday. A potter sits under a portico at the end of the Sante Fe Trail. She grabs a small stick to ring a terra cotta bell hung at her side. Her line of goods—cups, flowerpots, bowls, some glazed, some not. A Virgin Mary wearing a crown of bleached roses, dust accumulating in wrinkles of her garment. I dither in noon's sweat, leaning into the overhang shade. On a table next to her, a hand-built building—smaller than a breadbox without a roof. Dollhouse. Church. Saloon. Morphing playspace. A plastic bag inside holds round tables, chairs, an altar bar, a lamb, man and woman, cradle and donkey, an angel with abbreviated wings. At the bottom, a skeleton. I pay her. He has no advance directive.

Tricia Knoll (Williston, VT) is an aging poet who lives with two dogs in the woods of Vermont. Her work appears widely in journals, anthologies, and five collections. Two collections are forthcoming in 2023: *One Bent Twig* (Future Cycle Press) and *Wild Apples* (Fernwood Press). Tricia's 2018 *How I Learned To Be White* received the Human Relations Indie Book Award for Motivational Poetry. She is a Contributing Editor to *Verse-Virtual.*
triciaknoll.com

Flying in from O'Hare

Roberta Beary

The man crowding my armrest asks if I'm going home for Christmas. Do I have family in Phoenix? I nod. But don't say this is my first visit. Or that my brother has been in Arizona twenty years. Two hours later, I drive past my brother's house for the tenth time, thinking I must have the wrong address. Every dilapidated bungalow looks like a meth house, right down to the missing red roof tiles and dirt yards. How can he live here? My phone rings and I pull over. A fat and bald version of my brother is waving with one hand and putting his phone away with the other. He motions for me to pull into his driveway. We do an almost hug. I mumble, *Sorry for your loss*. My brother drags my suitcase inside. He throws it on a plastic beach chair. Says he wants to show me his horse. *I've got a little corral behind the house.*

> desert sunset
> the backdoor opens
> to empty bottles

We drive to the crematorium. A concrete chapel surrounded by palm trees. The distant hills look bloated, like my brother that Christmas twenty years back, when he promised to give up the booze for good. The chapel inside smells like sweet tea laced with ammonia. My brother takes a swig from his water bottle. I wonder what he's drinking. He tells me the world lost a good person and the Maricopa County sheriff got it wrong. Those five packets of meth taped in the wheel rim of my nephew's crushed car had nothing to do with him. *Why, he'd been clean for months.*

> giant cactus —
> strands of tinsel
> shape a crucifix

The man crowding the armrest asks if I'm going home for Christmas. Do I have family in Chicago? I nod. Close my eyes. See a makeshift corral framed by sloping hills. A white mare steps out of the twilight. *For a second I thought she'd run out on me too.* The man nudges my shoulder. *You were talking in your sleep,* he says.

Roberta Beary (Washington, DC / County Mayo, Ireland). Biographical note, page 69.

Dreams

John Macker

Years ago, when dissatisfied with them, I used to add a drone of menace. Now, they auger the sublime and the senseless. They sometimes whisper, *stop making sense* right before dawn. Good dreams beg to differ with the dystopia. Never boring, they never run out of color, they teach that beyond the weathered and the liminal is the horizon. They help to internalize the far reaches of dusk and love, and when foul weather ends, there are dustings of clarity, sometimes all the blood of the earth dries in the snow. My mother dances with William Holden in heaven, a rose between her teeth. Johnny Cash sings Trent Reznor in my shower. I've camped in a side canyon, serenaded by barn swallows on the far side of Mars. An anarchy of denizens: ghost dancers, rucksack poets, desert rats, Bashō, compañeros for the journey. Dream senses of place are replaced at dawn with wonder. A milagro. The world reimagines itself as unpolluted vistas and the warm coals of sunrise

> rivers bend away
> from long distance sleep
> the last things I hear

John Macker (Santa Fe, NM). Biographical note, page 14.

Home

Sarah Wolbach

Every week we bought firewood from an old man and his twisted twig of a son, the wood cut from shrinking forests in an ever-widening desert around San Miguel, stacked high on a tormented burro. In the remains of a Mexican hacienda once rowdy with scrawny dogs and children, we found generations of dust, tasted bitter peppercorns strewn beneath a tattered tree. Ruins everywhere we looked: in the faces of the old man and his son, in Mayan temples in the Yucatán, in abandoned silver mines near Guanajuato, in crumbling adobe dwellings in New Mexico, in derelict tenements of the Lower East Side. Fascinated by the echoes of disaster, we peered into wreckage, imagining it as our own. We moved often, from city to city, each move a harbinger of the ruin you would become over time, a disintegrating temple, a sinkhole of blood. In Santa Fe, gas exploded in the basement of our new house, cracking open the corner of your studio. Broken glass sprayed into the street and mingled with the soil in the garden. The wreck upended us. We found a new house, but your heart wasn't in it, and a pinched nerve eventually forced you into a wheelchair. No more clambering up ladders, as you once did in the ruins of Bandelier, climbing forty feet into the cliff dwellings of the Anasazi. *While I still can*, you said.

Sarah Wolbach (Santa Fe, NM). Biographical note, page 37.

Some Weeks after His Death

David Meischen

A final bend. The trail tunnels through tangled undergrowth to a band of muddy sand. The Rio Grande is wide and slow here. Sluggish, silted currents ripple around reedy sandbars—no hurry now. These waters rushed out of the San Juan Mountains, came tumbling through the ancient gorge's dizzy plunge. Down and down, slowing, broadening, to the flatness where I hug myself against January's gray chill. I'm facing east. The Sandias. Their hulking granite breaches skyward. A stirring of breeze shivers the stalks of last year's weedy abundance. The river glints and ripples.

> bolted sunflowers
> distant geese
> against winter sky

David Meischen (Albuquerque, NM). Biographical note, page 65.

Scott Wiggerman (Albuquerque, NM). Biographical note, page 16.

Hunting in the Bosque

Scott Wiggerman

No guns, no arrows. You're not out to kill anything. This hunt is entirely done through sight. You will need to flex your eyes, develop your ocular muscles, your depth perception. Be prepared to strain your neck backward, too. Yes, use binoculars if you must.

The best time to go is winter because the cottonwoods near the Rio Grande have lost their leaves: less camouflage, easier detection. Focus on the treetops. Yes, way up there. That clump that looks like an abandoned nest? Squint harder. This is what you're looking for: a porcupine. It's likely asleep, so may not move, its claws anchored to a branch that appears too thin for such a bundle. Yes, bigger than you think. A reason the French named them *spiny pigs*. Sometimes, you'll spot one shift just a smidge, but if you're lucky one may lumber into a crook.

After a while, the eyes adjust, and you will notice more porcupines with each hike, each in its own tree. You will wonder how you could have missed them on previous hikes. And if you need a souvenir, now is the time to look down. See the stripped bark at the tree's base, clawed and gnawed in savage slashes? Proof the porcupine eases down at night to forage. Now search the perimeter out from the trunk. Here's where, amidst the rotting leaves and scat on the forest floor, you might find a quill. This is your trophy.

art of the hunt
discovering
my feral side